Royal Jelly

A practical guide to the numerous ways
in which nature's richest health food
can help YOU!

Irene Stein, author of *Royal Jelly: A Guide to Nature's Richest Health Food.*

Royal Jelly

A guide to
nature's richest health food

IRENE STEIN

Illustrated by David Marsden

THORSONS PUBLISHING GROUP
Wellingborough · New York

First published March 1986
Second Impression June 1986

Note to reader

Before following the self-help advice given in this book readers are earnestly urged to give careful consideration to the nature of their particular health problem, and to consult a competent physician if in any doubt. This book should not be regarded as a substitute for professional medical treatment, and whilst every care is taken to ensure the accuracy of the content, the author and the publishers cannot accept legal responsibility for any problem arising out of the experimentation with the methods described.

British Library Cataloguing in Publication Data

Stein, Irene
    Royal jelly: a guide to nature's richest
    health food.
    1. Royal jelly — Physiological effect
    I. Title
    613.2'6   SF539

    ISBN 0-7225-1225-2

Printed and bound in Great Britain

CONTENTS

ACKNOWLEDGEMENTS

My thanks go to friends, colleagues and family. Without their interest, support and tolerance, I would not have been able to put these thoughts down on paper — thoughts about my approach to life and health which I have long wanted to share. Only with the help of those around me have I been able to fulfil this heartfelt ambition.

Thank you to Judy Quin, who left no phrase unturned in helping me to get my meaning across; to David Marsden, whose wonderful drawings, along with my daily dose of Royal Jelly, help me to look at life with a chuckle; to Gerry Simler, my friend who crossed every 't' and dotted every 'i' in his concern for the success of this book; to Duncan and Louise who checked, double-checked and encouraged me; to my daughters Lisa and Jane for putting up with ceaseless Royal Jelly talk; to Cheryse, Vicki, Mary, Elizabeth, Enzian, Rio, Steve, Girish and Sylvana, the remainder of my dedicated team, who help me daily to bring Royal Jelly's health-giving properties to others.

I'm sure none of them will take it amiss if I reserve my greatest thanks for the Honey Bee, without whom not only my book, but the life I love, would not have been possible.

FOREWORD

About eleven years ago an alternative practitioner recommended I take Royal Jelly and I've been taking it ever since.

People often ask me how I manage to look so fit. Although I always tell them that I believe I owe my good health and fitness to Royal Jelly, I actually find it difficult to go into long explanations. If I do, then people tend to say, 'If it's as good as all that, why haven't I heard of it before?'

So, I was very pleased when Irene asked me to write a few words of introduction to her book. If you've decided to read it, then I assume you must be sympathetic to the 'health through nature' approach to life. I therefore welcome this opportunity to tell you of my own experience.

My life may appear to be fairly glamorous, I suppose, but it all really comes down to hard work. There's rehearsing and performing — sometimes more than one show a day — and I am also asked to appear at all sorts of functions and social events. When I'm not working, I'm probably windsurfing or skin-diving, or just relaxing with the family. One capsule containing 150mg of fresh Royal Jelly taken each day with my morning cup of tea — that, I'm convinced, is what keeps me cheerful and full of energy, and gives me the capacity to enjoy everything I do to the full, even when I have a heavy schedule to contend with.

Quite a lot of my friends and colleagues are on Royal Jelly, too, and Vicky, my wife, swears by it. One thing we both find is that fresh Royal Jelly keeps our weight stable. Also, we never seem to suffer from colds and other minor infections.

As for the liquid version of fresh Royal Jelly, I find it very helpful. Naturally, even I have days when I'm not sure I'm going to stand the pace. On stage you need energy and stamina, but most of all you need concentration; a phial of Royal Jelly appears to put me in the right frame of mind and to help me right through to the end of the show.

It's a pity so many people resort to pep pills and drugs when there are natural products like Royal Jelly which can bring good health, a sense of well-being and the ability to cope with everyday problems.

The day I walked into that surgery, my health and my nerves were in a fairly terrible state. I never thought I'd be telling you, eleven years later, how great I feel. So now, for once, I really have told the whole story of how I apparently manage to look so fit. I'm glad to have the chance of helping Irene to share her knowledge and enthusiasm for Royal Jelly with you.

JOE BROWN

INTRODUCTION

Like many books, this one is the result of a personal obsession. Since I discovered Royal Jelly in 1974, as everyone around me will tell you, I *have* been obsessed by it. The study of its therapeutic potential, its development as an aid to physical and mental health, and the increase of its popularity and availability, have pervaded my personal as well as my professional life ever since.

Within days of starting my regime of one 150mg capsule a day, I felt fitter, healthier, livelier and more confident than I had ever felt before. The difference in my state of mind and body was so striking that I could hardly believe it. I decided, therefore, to get a hundred people to start taking Royal Jelly to see if their reactions would be as overwhelming as mine.

Here are a few examples of the results.

One woman's varicose veins were so bad that she had been wearing bandages for seven years. After taking Royal Jelly for only two months, off came the bandages.

A man with a duodenal ulcer had reached the stage where an operation seemed to be the only course of action. The hospital waiting list was long, and in the meantime he was in considerable discomfort. He began his Royal Jelly regime, and before his turn came round, he was better. Just to prove the point, he prepared himself an enormous 'fry-up' of all the fatty foods he had had to avoid for years! He never did have that operation, and he's still healthy today.

A quite severe stroke had affected one of my human 'guinea pigs' very badly. He found this particularly frustrating, because he was unable to complete the book he had just begun writing. After a couple of months on Royal Jelly, he got up and finished his task. He also reported one side-effect which he hadn't counted on, but which was none the less welcome. His sexual desires (and performance) were greatly enhanced!

One elderly woman was so emotionally disturbed and neurotic that she had lost the will to live. She simply stared into space all day and all night long. On Royal Jelly, she gradually started to lead a normal life again, learnt to drive and was able to get a good night's sleep for the first time in years.

A young man was always in and out of prison because his violent temper and his drink problem combined to get him repeatedly into trouble. Royal Jelly calmed him and cured his desire to drink and today he is a happy family man.

A friend with a fluid retention problem had been taking diuretics for five years. The cause of the condition had not been identified and the treatment had produced inconsistent results. After taking Royal Jelly for just four days, she noticed a significant improvement.

These and many other almost incredible stories which resulted from my informal trial naturally increased my enthusiasm for the product. I began to import and distribute Royal Jelly and to make it available to the general public through practitioners, health food stores and beauty salons. At this time, fresh Royal Jelly capsules only had a shelf-life of three months, because of the nature of the capsule shell. I commissioned research which resulted in the development of a capsule which was completely airtight. Since scientists have proved that fresh Royal Jelly is more potent than the processed variety, I felt that this work was important — I wanted fresh Royal Jelly to be easily available to as many people as possible.

Since then I have been instrumental in formulating several fresh Royal Jelly based products for internal as well as external application, and today Royal Jelly's fame has spread so far that I am exporting it to over forty countries. In parts of the South of France, people take Royal Jelly as a matter of course. In the

Arabic countries, it is regarded as an aphrodisiac as well as a health-booster. In parts of the USA, there are people of a particular Christian sect who feel Royal Jelly is 'god-given'. And there are practitioners of every possible discipline and persuasion all over the world prescribing Royal Jelly for the alleviation of specific disorders as well as for increasing general health and well-being.

As you will see from the following pages, the 'almost incredible stories' continue to pour in. All the letters and testimonials which I have quoted from in this book are genuine. I have copies of them all and they are available for inspection.

It is partly due to this endorsement by others that my commitment to Royal Jelly goes from strength to strength. My personal response to the substance and that of my family over the years is probably, however, the real driving force behind my continuing 'obsession'.

After some twelve years of taking Royal Jelly every day, I look younger than when I started. Friends comment on this when they see old photos of me. At the ripe old age of forty-seven, my skin tone is the envy of many people a good deal younger than me. My hairdresser tells me that, despite regular highlighting, my hair is amazingly healthy.

After a recent hysterectomy, the rate of my recovery was phenomenal. On two capsules, three times a day, I was back at work in a week and driving after a fortnight, and my scar practically vanished in no time.

In my youth, I was always visiting the dentist. Yet now, when I go for my check-up, the verdict is always the same — no treatment required. I never get a cold, and any virus which I may pick up, I shake off almost immediately.

I could go on and on about the physical benefits of Royal Jelly to me, but perhaps most interesting of all are the psychological, emotional and intellectual benefits.

I lead a busy life with a family and home to run as well as my own business. I also find time for tennis, weight training, Life Training, and a busy social life. I don't just 'cope' with this, as many women have to these days; I actively enjoy every moment.

Stamina, mental competence, memory for detail, a positive attitude in a crisis, the ability to remain alert despite lack of sleep. In my pre-Royal Jelly period, this description of my capabilities would have raised a scoffing laugh among my friends and colleagues. Perhaps maturity has something to do with this 'mental expansion', but I attribute it to Royal Jelly.

My mother, Sophie, is seventy-six, and on Royal Jelly she looks twenty years younger. At the age of sixty-five, she couldn't even walk properly, let alone run. She was crippled with arthritis. Now there's no trace of it.

My children, too, have been on the regime since they were eight and ten respectively. Before then, Lisa was an ailing child, frequently absent from school with coughs, colds and earache. After starting on Royal Jelly, she never had a day off school. Jane, too has benefitted from our family regime. You wouldn't know to look at her that she has recently recovered from extensive and painful surgery. The speed of her healing and recovery brought incredulous comments from her medical team.

Naturally, there are many people who take Royal Jelly who do not have spectacular stories to tell. The problem is that once you get used to feeling good, you tend to take it for granted. Many people have stopped taking it for this reason, but most of them are back for new supplies within months. There are others who try to remain sceptical and don't admit to feeling any particular benefit, yet they keep taking the capsules. If I had been given a fiver each time I've heard the phrase, 'I don't know if it's the Royal Jelly, but . . .', I'd probably be a millionaire.

In my research for this book, I have found that there is more to Royal Jelly than even I suspected. I hope, by sharing this information and some of my thoughts on what I feel is an enlightened approach to good health, I can cause a little of my enthusiasm to rub off on you.

1.
BEES DO IT

The honey-bee has fascinated scientists, philosophers and poets for centuries. It is indeed a unique and intriguing creature. The life of the bee colony has been studied from many different points of view. I have observed that, however subjective or detached their accounts might be, most students find it difficult *not* to include in their descriptions some allusion to human society. In his *Ascent of Man*, Professor Jacob Bronowski describes life in the hive as,

> a totalitarian paradise, for ever loyal, for ever fixed, because it has shut itself off from the adventure of diversity that drives and changes the higher animals and man.

On looking up the honey-bee in a cherished set of encyclopaedias which belonged to my father, published in the 'thirties, I found this description:

> Honey-bees are perfect socialists; they labour without competition or personal reward.

The colony consists of one queen, several hundred drones, and between 25,000 and 100,000 workers. As bees die off constantly, the queen may in one season become the mother of a quarter of a million bees. It has been shown that the development of the bodily structure, physiology and metabolism which makes this staggering reproductive capacity possible depends on diet, and the queen is fed exclusively on Royal Jelly. Sometimes known as 'bees milk', this whitish solution is secreted by the glands of worker bees of a certain age.

Worker bees are females which develop from fertilized eggs. They themselves are infertile and very aptly named; among the worker bees' duties are cleaning and ventilating the hive, gathering pollen, collecting nectar and turning it into honey, gorging themselves with honey in order to produce wax for building the honeycomb, defending the hive, and feeding the larvae as well as their queen.

Perhaps the most anthropomorphic description of hive life is that of Maurice Maeterlinck in his *Life of the Bee*. It is unashamedly romantic. Yet I find his description of the hapless worker compelling and, at the same time, informative. He sees the force which drives the workers to perform these tasks when the needs arise as the 'Spirit of the Hive'.

It regulates the workers' labours, with due regard to their age; it allots their tasks to the nurses who tend the nymphs and their larvae, the ladies of honour who wait on the queen, and never allow her out of their sight; the house bees who air, refresh, or heat the hive by fanning their wings, and hasten the evaporation of the honey that may be too highly charged with water; the architects, masons, waxworkers and sculptors who form the chain and construct the combs; the foragers who sally forth to the flowers in search of the nectar that turns into honey, of the pollen that feeds the nymphs and the larvae, the propolis that welds and strengthens the buildings of the city, or the water and salt required by the youth of the nation. Its orders have gone to the chemists, who ensure the preservation of the honey by letting a drop of formic acid fall in from the end of their string; to the capsule makers, who seal down the cells when the treasure is ripe; to the sweepers, who maintain public places and streets most irreproachably clean; to the bearers, whose duty it is to remove the corpses; and to the amazons of the guard who keep watch on the threshold by day and by night, question comers and goers, recognize the novices who return from their very first flight, scare away vagabonds, marauders, and the loiterers, expel all intruders, attack redoubtable foes in a body, and, if need be, barricade the entrance.

It is no wonder that in order to carry out some of these demanding and varied services, the worker's anatomy also possesses some very special features.

Each one has inside her body three specialized glands which, in human terms, are very complex chemical laboratories. One of these produces honey, another converts honey into wax, and the third manufactures Royal Jelly.

The worker bees are one of the three 'castes' into which adult bees are divided. Yet the queen lays only two types of eggs — fertilized and unfertilized. After mating, only once, with a drone, in mid-air, she is capable of storing his sperms. If she releases an egg on its own, without a sperm, it develops into a drone — a male whose sole purpose in his short life is to fertilize a queen. If, however, she releases a fertilized egg, it has the potential to develop into either of the two types of adult female — a worker or a queen.

The worker is a fascinating insect, as we have already seen, but she only grows to about half the size of her sovereign, lives for a mere six weeks at most, and is incapable of reproduction.

The queen is not only much larger and heavier. *Her* lifespan can be as long as six *years* and, although her output varies with the seasons, she lays up to *2,000 eggs a day.*

So, from larvae which are identical, two very different creatures evolve, each one highly specialized for her role within the colony.

In addition to the glands I have already mentioned, the worker honey-bee possesses a brain which is much larger than that of her queen. Each of her hind legs incorporates combs for collecting pollen from her body, a tiny press with which to compact the pollen, and baskets to store it in. She has a very versatile mouth arrangement which allows her to draw nectar from flowers, chew pollen, manipulate wax and attack intruders.

The queen, on the other hand, develops an ovipositor through which she lays her eggs, and a sperm storage sac in her abdomen. She has none of the food-gathering and conversion equipment and she is, in fact, incapable of feeding herself.

A close study of the dietary arrangements in the hive provides the key with which to unlock this apparent mystery of how two creatures with such widely and startlingly different anatomical structures and physiological functions can emerge from identical sets of genetic information.

For three days after the white bee larvae hatch from their eggs, they are all fed on Royal Jelly. This milky secretion certainly does not *look* very appetizing. Yet it contains *all* the amino acids as well as ten vitamins and six minerals. It is by observing what happens next, and by trying a little interference with nature, that apiologists have identified just what it is that causes this unique phenomenon.

Long and painstaking observations have shown that the egg which is destined to rule as queen is placed in a large acorn-shaped cell. The egg whose lot is to be that of a worker is placed in a cell which measures about half a centimetre (1/5 inch) long.

Now here's the astonishing evidence for Royal Jelly as a queen-maker. Switch the larvae, and whichever one is placed in the queen cell, as long as this experimental changeover is carried out in the first three days, becomes a queen. Whichever one is placed in the worker cell becomes a worker.

Surely it couldn't be the shape and size of the cell which was the determining factor?

The scientists looked further. They examined the way in which the nurse worker bees treated each type of cell. They discovered that Royal Jelly is supplied to the queen cell throughout the larval stage, and, in fact, that it continues throughout the queen bee's life. Wherever she goes in the hive, workers turn towards her and lick her body. On their tongues is the supply of Royal Jelly, and in this way the queen is able to absorb it. It is this exclusive treatment which emerges as the trigger and the sustainer of separate development.

On the fourth day after hatching, the supply of Royal Jelly is cut off from the larvae in the worker cells. They continue to be reared on a dilute solution of pollen and nectar. Once

this dietary change has taken place, these larvae are denied the royal mantle.

Leave a bee grub in a worker cell for just one day after its Royal Jelly supply is suspended, and, even if you transfer it to a queen cell and its royal diet is restored, it still does not become a queen. It does not achieve the size, the longevity or the phenomenal fertility of the queen bee.

The honey-bee has long been respected and cherished for its supply of honey. The discovery of Royal Jelly has stimulated new and intensified investigations over the last forty years or so into life within the hive. As these continue, and the full analysis and potential of this substance are gradually revealed, the reputation of this remarkable insect is not only endorsed, but greatly enhanced.

2.
WHAT'S IN IT FOR US?

Diet is evidently crucial to the anatomical and physical development of each bee, to the continuation of each colony and, indeed, to the survival of the species itself. But how important is *our* diet to the well-being of the human race?

Surprisingly recently in our own civilization, people were dying of scurvy, and rickets was a deforming disease. If someone had told our great grandfathers that these could be cured and even prevented by a change of diet, he would probably have been dismissed, as fanciful at best — at worst as a dangerous crank. Yet, with the discovery and isolation of vitamins and an appreciation of their value to the human metabolism, these are just two of the savage disorders which have been eradicated from western civilization, simply by changing the menu.

Adjusting the diet to promote good health and prolong life is a notion which should, then, find favour with us all.

There is no substitute for a varied diet containing as many different nutrient elements as possible. If we could find our way through the maze of advice which is so freely available today and then have the time and the freedom to follow the best of it to the letter, doctors' surgeries, as well as hospitals, would, I suppose, be less crowded.

It is my firm and lasting conviction that getting the dietary balance right is the *first* line approach to good health and well-being — not, as it is so often regarded, something to try when 'conventional' therapies fail.

Let me illustrate what I mean. I mentioned the lack of

A change of menu can promote better health.

freedom to choose what we eat. A friend of mine complained bitterly when I visited her in hospital recently, after the birth of her second baby. 'They bring us plastic bread and all manner of processed foods. Then, each evening, the nurse asks me, "Have you opened your bowels today, dear?" When I guiltily reply, "No," I am offered a laxative to do the trick.' 'Now,' my friend continued, 'If they gave us a decent diet, we might all function naturally!'

It's funny how hospital visiting chit-chat often seems to turn to the same old topic — but my friend has a valid point. Hospitalization is a specific example of how our choice of diet can be limited, yet the demands of our daily routine and other circumstances restrict most of us a lot of the time.

Also, many people deliberately banish certain foods from their tables, because of religious or other conscientious and heartfelt principles.

Diet supplements, especially those derived from natural sources, which can help restore the balance, therefore deserve serious consideration, and their use is gaining popularity by the day.

Royal Jelly is a substance which researchers have found well worth analysing. [1] Its composition is extremely complex, and many of the scientific papers which have been published can only be understood by other scientists! About four per cent of its make up has so far defied analysis, and this is probably why attempts at copying Royal Jelly synthetically have failed. Just as there is no perfect substitute for breast milk, there isn't one for fresh Royal Jelly either.

Let me take the major elements which *have* been identified and briefly describe the role these constituents play in the *human* metabolism.

The Vitamins

Vitamins are organic substances essential for the normal functioning of the body. One of the main reasons for their remaining undetected for so long is that they are required in such tiny amounts.

It was a man named Funk who coined the word 'vitamin' in 1911, from 'vita', the latin for 'life' and 'amine', meaning 'a chemical compound'. No wonder he named them so, for without them we cannot digest and utilize the fats, proteins, carbohydrates and minerals present in our diet. They help to form enzymes which convert food into energy. Vitamins also play a major role in the body's defence mechanism, protecting us against disease, infection and environmental stress.

Those which are present in Royal Jelly are vitamins B_1, B_2, B_3, B_5, B_6, B_7, B_8, B_9, B_{12}, and vitamin C.

Vitamin B_1 or thiamin is essential for the conversion of carbohydrates into energy. It is no surprise, then, that a lack of energy is among the symptoms which can result from a severe lack of vitamin B_1 in the diet.

Poor digestion and (as my friend in hospital would testify) constipation can also be caused by insufficient intake of vitamin B_1, as can headaches, heart trouble, a bad complexion and loss of appetite.

Many people claim that a regular intake of Royal Jelly has helped to rid them of one, or several, of these troublesome and often distressingly serious problems.

A Hertfordshire businessman writes,

As a longtime sufferer of headaches I was quite amazed to find that since taking it (Royal Jelly) I have not suffered, to any great extent, from headaches.

A practitioner of 'alternative' medicine in Surrey writes,

Debility, chest infections, liver and stomach problems have all responded quickly to Royal Jelly . . .'

Vitamin B_2, also known as riboflavin, is a component of various enzymes which are concerned in the transport around the body of hydrogen and electrons. A deficiency of this vitamin can cause cracked, rough skin and inflamed, sore eyes.

It is tempting with symptoms of this kind to begin by treating them externally — the skin perhaps with expensive face creams and the eyes with drops which purport to put the sparkle back. These preparations can have a soothing effect, but B_2 in the diet will genuinely alleviate the problems, and, of course, help to prevent them from arising in the first place.

Many people report improvements in their skin after taking Royal Jelly for a time. Here is the testimony of a nurse in Watford.

So I tried Royal Jelly treatment . . . my skin is much improved and not so dry.

A housewife from the Midlands relates,

Usually at this time of year my face feels dry, taut and flaky, but all the time I have used (Royal Jelly) it has felt marvellous.

A lack of **vitamin B$_3$**, known also as vitamin P-P, or niacin, results in pellagra, a serious disease marked by digestive disorder, dermatitis and neurological disturbance. It was not until the late 1930s that this vitamin was finally identified as the 'pellagra-preventive' (P-P). Although this breakthrough is now part of medical history, there are still people in America who succumb to the disease. The reason is an enforced lack of variety in the diet through poverty.

Royal Jelly is also rich in **vitamin B$_5$** or pantothenic acid, which aids the metabolism of carbohydrates, fats and proteins and is associated with the prolongation of life.

Many elderly people feel that they derive great benefit from Royal Jelly. Particularly, they report the alleviation or total disappearance of many ailments which afflict us as we grow older.

Experiments carried out in Paris by Dr Betourne, with injected Royal Jelly, also demonstrate a hopeful future for it as an aid in the field of geriatric medicine. The general comment of his colleague, Dr Chauvin, is that these tests

> tend to prove that Royal Jelly has most salutary results in cases of debility and senility. Improvement becomes noticeable after only a few injections (and) seems lasting.[2]

It is not so much as a rejuvenator that Royal Jelly has received a great deal of publicity, but rather as an agent which appears to arrest or, at least, slow down the process of ageing. Many people, including some well known personalities, famous for their apparent perennial youth, believe that Royal Jelly keeps them young, energetic and full of vitality, despite the advancing years. At least one testimonial on this subject is worth printing in full.

> I would like to tell you that I have been taking Royal Jelly for ten years. I have always thought that it gave me a feeling of well-being and was good for me.
> Recently I had my thoughts confirmed by a visit from an old

friend, who had not seen me for that length of time. We both had a shock. In those ten years she had aged and wrinkled considerably, having been through any number of minor ailments that had lowered her resistance.

She told me that she had expected me to have aged as she had, and was surprised that I hadn't. In fact if anything she found me looking younger and more positive than the last time she saw me. She added that I was more like the young woman she had met twenty years ago.

Vitamin B$_6$, also known as pyridoxine, is important to the metabolism of amino acids which are needed for growth, repair and replacement of tissues. Since Royal jelly has also been discovered to contain all known amino acids, I shall be discussing *their* importance later. Without B$_6$, though, the body would be incapable of using them.

Vitamin B$_7$, or inositol, is vital for hair growth, the metabolism of fats and the efficient functioning of the vital organs. Many people who take regular doses of Royal Jelly report unusually rapid hair growth, and all of them feel generally healthier, with a renewed sense of well-being and vitality.

Vitamin B$_8$, or biotin, is involved in the metabolism of carbohydrates, proteins and fats. It also helps keep hormones in balance and plays an important role in keeping skin and hair in good condition.

Vitamin B$_9$ (folic acid) and **B$_{12}$** (cobalamin, the only vitamin to contain a mineral — cobalt) are both essential for the production and maintenance of healthy blood. A severe deficiency of B$_9$ can cause megaloblastic anaemia in which the red blood cells become abnormally large, whereas a lack of B$_{12}$ can result in pernicious anaemia and disorders of the nervous system. It affects, particularly, the cells producing blood in the bone marrow and the cells in the digestive tract.

For vegetarians, a supplement of B$_{12}$ is regarded by many as indispensable, since the usual source is the soil — this unique vitamin, with its trace of cobalt, being passed to us via the food chain in meat.

Naturally, as we rely on the blood to transport oxygen and nutrients to all parts of the body and to dispose of carbon dioxide and waste products on its return journey, healthy blood is crucial to general good health and well-being.

Now we come to perhaps the most famous of all the vitamins, **vitamin C.** The fact that it is universally recognized as so important is probably because without enough of it, the entire structure of the human body would disintegrate. It produces the material which actually holds the cells of the body together to form tissues and organs. Vitamin C is needed for the maintenance of blood-vessels, muscles, cartilage, strong bones and teeth and healthy lungs, for the production of red blood cells and the healing of wounds. Its action is so complex and so fundamental to the human metabolism, that a complete list of its roles would fill a book on its own.

One of the problems with vitamin C is that it is highly unstable. Cooking destroys a high percentage of a food's original content and can eliminate it altogether. Exposing fruit and vegetables to the air and even cutting them with a metal knife can reduce their vitamin C content. So, even a conscientious effort to ensure the inclusion of enough vitamin C in your diet can be frustrated.

The Amino Acids
Thirty of these occur in nature, and Royal Jelly has been discovered to contain them all! Eight of them are known as 'essential', not because the rest are less important, but because the body itself can manufacture them from other materials. These eight, however, can only be supplied by the diet. Their source is animal protein. A dietary supplement such as Royal Jelly which contains these crucial substances is of special value to vegetarians.

Amino acids are the constituent parts of proteins and play a significant role in producing energy for physical activity and the maintenance of vital functions. They are also associated with protection and resistance to disease. Their main function is as body-building nutrients; they are responsible for growth, repair and replacement of tissues.

The more I delve into the workings of the human body, the more their complexity and the interaction of the various nutrients which keep us alive and well strike me as almost unfathomable. It's no wonder that even doctors within a particular medical discipline commonly disagree. It is difficult, therefore, to connect some of the beliefs and claims of people who take Royal Jelly to the presence of an isolated constituent of this rich substance. A few extracts from what they say, however, do echo some of the points I have made in these paragraphs on vitamins and amino acids.

A Welsh lady who had suffered from arthritis, particularly in the spine and legs, and who turned to Royal Jelly in desperation, found she could enjoy an active holiday for the first time in many years. She writes,

> I walked up and down the hilly streets of Falmouth with little difficulty and hardly any breathlessness — something which would have been impossible a few months ago.

A London woman testifies,

> I started taking the Jelly last January and I just cannot believe the results. I have had no pain in my toes since last May.

This comment comes from County Cork:

> I have (or rather had) psoriasis of the scalp . . . but since I have been taking Royal Jelly it has completely disappeared.

A grateful Mum in New Zealand says,

> Matthew's been taking it (Royal Jelly) every day since early summer. He started Kindergarten in September. He has caught two colds, but the great thing is that he recuperated without antibiotics. It's the first time in three years that his body has had the strength to fight an infection.

From North London:

> After three days of taking (500mg of Royal Jelly) I noticed the small scar I had from the operation almost healed and was not even sore.

The variety of the benefits which people feel they gain from taking Royal Jelly seems almost infinite. Here is the disappearance of yet another disorder which a lady from Surrey attributes to the product:

> After two months supply of Royal Jelly I have been free of cystitis completely. I have been plagued with this for five years.

A Nottingham woman relates,

> I like the Royal Jelly. I have an illness which causes fluid retention and found it very good for reducing it.

A sportswoman of international standing writes,

> I have benefitted enormously from taking it (Royal Jelly); I find extra reserves of energy for my very active life and have an overall feeling of vitality and well-being.

While I'm on the subject of energy and stamina, an American ultra-distance runner claims,

> It has been two months since I started taking Royal Jelly. In the 100 K race, I bettered my last year's time by thirty-four minutes without even trying.

The Minerals
About four per cent of our body weight is accounted for by minerals which, just like all the other nutrients, must be supplied by the diet. Minerals do not provide energy themselves, but since they form an integral part of the tissues and the skeleton, they are needed for growth. Some are needed

Many athletes report easier training and improved performance.

in relatively large amounts and are known as *macro-elements* and although others are only needed in minute quantities, or *traces*, they act as catalysts and carriers and are therefore indispensable to the normal functioning of the body.

Royal Jelly contains six minerals, they are sodium, potassium, iron, chromium, manganese and nickel.

About thirty per cent of the sodium in the body is in the bones. The rest, which is in fluids such as plasma and the extracellular fluids of nerve and muscle tissue, is responsible for regulating the water balance of the body. The other *macro-element* contained in Royal Jelly is potassium, which works in partnership with the sodium from inside the cell walls. At the two extremes, both dehydration and severe swelling, or oedema, can result from a breakdown of fluid control, as many people know, fluid retention can be a problem, especially for the elderly, the pregnant and the overweight!

It is no accident that iron is perhaps the most well known of the *trace elements*. It is one of the few minerals which are classified as essential. That means that deficiencies can occur and when they do, serious disorders can result. Seventy per cent of the iron in the body is in the haemoglobin, the most important component of the red blood cells. It gives blood its red colour and is responsible for the transport of oxygen to all parts of the body.

Chromium, manganese and nickel are also important to the metabolism, and although they are required in relatively tiny quantities, today's processed foods often fail to supply these *trace elements*.

All in all, after reading even this somewhat cursory analysis of just some of the components of food and their value to our metabolism, I do not believe that anyone could dismiss the vital importance of a balanced diet. I hope, too, that I have helped to demonstrate that, in the list of alternative ways in which we can approach healing, the adjustment of diet deserves a place at the top.

As far as Royal Jelly is concerned, the scientific community has well and truly demonstrated that it contains a phenomenal number of elements which are literally vital to our existence.

References

1. A sample of researches which have been conducted in order to determine the composition of larval food: A. Planta,

(1898, 1899); R. Elser, (1929); W. Rhein, (1933); G. F. Townsend and C. C. Lucass, (1940); M. K. Haydak, (1943); J. E. J. Habovsky and R. W. Shuel, (1959); N. G. Patel et al, (1960, 1961); M. H. Haydak, (1961); I. Jung-Hoffman, (1966, 1968); N. Weaver et al, (1968); J. Pain, (1968); M. H. Haydak, (1968); R. Boch et al, (1979); J. Beetsma, (1979); H. Rembold, (1980); K. Weiss, (1980, 1981); A. T. Thrasyvoulou et al, (1983).

2. R. Chauvin, 'Action sur les Mammiferes et sur l'Homme de la gelee royale' (*L'Apiculteur, Sect. Scientif.,* 101 Annee No. 4, April 1957).

3.
TAKE IT EASY

A varied diet is, as I believe everyone would agree, preferable to taking pills and potions. Nevertheless, whether for reasons of culinary convenience or simply because the 'right' foods are not always readily available, most of us do resort to processed foods of various kinds.

It has been shown beyond doubt that processing of any sort can diminish not only the quantity, but also the *quality* of the vitamins and proteins contained in the original foodstuff. When it comes to pills which are designed to supplement those elements which are commonly deficient in our diet, many of them contain artificial substitutes which are chemically produced, and therefore do not compare with the real thing in terms of quality. Now that it is possible to turn naturally occurring nutrients into a convenient form for us to take, we can obtain supplementary nutrition of a higher calibre.

'Health through Nature' is more than just a slogan. We all know by now that we can restore and retain better health levels by just looking after ourselves. The simple set of rules looks down at us from hoardings, stares up at us from press ads, and is promoted by the Health Education Council and other bodies. Eat sensibly, don't smoke and take a little exercise. If we all followed this advice, we'd be in better shape and we might prevent certain disorders from setting in in later life. We might also do our bit in reducing the drugs bill for the National Health.

As for exercise, as long as each person is wary of overdoing things and only jogs, or walks, or does aerobics, or spends time in the gym, to a level which feels good, yet comfortable, these activities can help with circulation, respiration, digestion and mental stress. The only thing which may be weak is the flesh. But if you miss your morning run because you can't be bothered, or if you can't go to your keep-fit class because the babysitter lets you down, you can always get off the bus or the train a few stops earlier or leave your car and walk for a change.

Not smoking can be more difficult for many. Fortunately the number of habitual smokers is decreasing literally by the day. It's not a problem I've had to face myself, but I do know that nagging rarely helps. The decision to stop has to come from within, and even then the going isn't easy. Even hardened smokers of my acquaintance have, however, been helped by the 'No smoking days' campaign, and so the picture isn't all bleak.

Then we come to eating sensibly, and, as I have said, if you can't get all the nutrients your body needs from your diet, then try to seek the most natural substitute you can. Royal Jelly is, of course, natural. Exactly how the worker bee turns its raw materials of pollen and nectar into this protein, vitamin and mineral-rich substance has been under investigation for some time, and no complete answer has been found. Bits of the jigsaw are beginning to appear, though. For example, in *Bee World* Johansson writes,

> The vitamin (B_5, or pantothenic acid) in bee milk might be obtained from the digestion by nurse bees of protein in pollen, or as a by-product of intermediary metabolism involving phosphatase action in the blood or pharyngeal gland.

Another scientist, Goto, postulates that the biotin *d*-sulphoxide is produced by oxidation of the biotin in pollen eaten by worker bees . . . And so it goes on! Suffice it to say that an attempt has been made to reproduce Royal Jelly synthetically, and when this substitute was used in medical trials, it did not produce the encouraging results which were obtained with the real

thing.[1]. So, it seems that if we want to benefit from the technology of the honey-bee, there is no other way than to gather the fruits of the worker bees' labours from the hive itself.

Scientists have established that Royal Jelly possesses marked bactericidal properties, even greater than those found in some carbolic acid compounds, which have long been used as components of disinfectants and antiseptics. It can, therefore, be kept for long periods without spoiling.

Many manufacturers of commercial Royal Jelly products find it convenient to lyophilize (freeze-dry) the substance, once it is extracted from the hive, since it is then easier to handle and to put into capsules which can be swallowed. It has been demonstrated, however, that even this freeze-drying process can lessen the *quality* of the nutrients contained in Royal Jelly, thus reducing the potential benefits which the components may offer. I shall be discussing this aspect of commercially available Royal Jelly in a later chapter.

You can get pure fresh Royal Jelly in a jar, to be taken by the spoonful. It is a slightly viscous yellowish-white liquid which looks quite unappetizing, smells odd and tastes fairly peculiar to most palates — and the after-taste is something else! A friend of mine described it as 'very ripe cheese'. Yet really staunch Royal Jelly fans take a small spoonful of this substance every day.

Most people favour either the capsule form, which can easily be swallowed, or products in which the Royal Jelly is blended with more palatable ingredients. Both of these also provide the manufacturer with the opportunity to add to nature's recipe by including other substances, either for the manufacturer's own convenience, for example preservatives or colourings, or for the consumer's benefit, for example nature's own ingredients such as herbs, honey, pollen and added natural vitamins.

Recently, a product has also been developed for the external application of Royal Jelly as a cream, making its nutritional properties directly available to the skin.

Royal Jelly Capsules

The shell of most Royal Jelly capsules is made of gelatin, and those containing freeze-dried Royal Jelly may also include soya bean oil, hydrogenated vegetable oil, beeswax, stabilizer, soya lecithin and other extracts and additives.

There is one brand of capsule on the market which contains Royal Jelly in its fresh state. The technology which had to be developed to encapsulate the product straight from the hive makes this type of product more expensive, but, as I have already mentioned, and as I shall discuss later in more depth, many people feel that the preservation of the purity of the Royal Jelly, and hence the potency of its constituents, justifies the extra outlay.

Whether freeze-dried or fresh, the usual amount of Royal Jelly in each capsule is between 100 and 150mg. The capsules are designed as a continuous regime of one capsule a day. Some manufacturers recommend that it be taken first thing on an empty stomach and others say it should be taken with food. The intention is gradually to restore the proper balance of nutrients within the body, so that the metabolism can reach its optimum performance. In this way each person can achieve his or her maximum level of general health. Very few claim miracles for Royal Jelly, yet once an individual's full capacity for good health is reached, within the limitations of his or her general condition, the consequent feeling of well-being, often coupled with relief from minor ailments, and the symptoms of quite serious disorders, can seem miraculous.

It is quite common for a person who begins to use Royal Jelly capsules not to notice the general but gradual improvement which in most cases begins to take place. Frequently, once you have begun your Royal Jelly programme, the first signs that your body is changing are comments from friends, colleagues and relatives who begin to say how fit you look, how bright you seem and how radiant your complexion is. It's rather like watching a child grow. If you are with him every day, the change is so gradual, that it is in itself imperceptible until he makes a breakthrough, like one day reaching the light-switch or the door-handle. Yet, those who see him only occasionally almost invariably comment on how he has grown, and how he has changed.

With women, once the regime is established, the first milestone is often a comment from their hairdressers, when they see a change in the condition of the hair and can stop using conditioners. Usually, the next manifestation of the healthier being is stronger nails. No more sitting on the hands or using special varnishes and other preparations, and no more swearing as another carefully nurtured work of art and dedication bites the dust.

Most suppliers of Royal Jelly capsules would recommend that a course of at least two or three months should be tried

before the subject can begin to assess in full whether a better standard of health, a greater feeling of well-being, as well as an improved ability to cope with life, are emerging.

It is a regime of 150mg of fresh Royal Jelly per day in capsule form which has produced volumes of reaction from people who have made it part of their lives. General descriptions of enjoying better health, feeling and looking more beautiful, and coping more efficiently with the stress of life, abound. In addition to that, here is a comprehensive list of the ailments, disorders and diseases which have, according to the authors of these testimonies, been eradicated or alleviated by Royal Jelly capsules:

Acne, allergies, anaemia, angina, anorexia, anxiety, arthritis, asthma, baldness, breathlessness, bronchitis, cancer, colds, constipation, coronary disease, cramp, cystitis, debility, depression, dermatitis, dysmenorrhoea, dyspepsia, eczema, fatigue, haemorrhoids, hay-fever, headaches, hernia, herpes, hyperactivity, hypertension, hypotension, impotence, insomnia, malnutrition, muscular dystrophy, nausea, neurosis, pain, phlebitis, post-natal depression, pre-menstrual tension, psoriasis, respiratory disorders and varicose veins.

Many also feel that Royal Jelly capsules have helped them to cope with various problems during certain periods of their lives, including adolescence, pregnancy and breast-feeding, and the menopause. Certain drugs and excesses can result in extra nutritional requirements, too, and people taking oral contraceptives as well as people drinking a little more alcohol than they should have found relief from the side-effects of these activities through taking Royal Jelly capsules regularly.

Royal Jelly and Honey
Because a significant portion of the population dislike or cannot swallow capsules — for example, children and the elderly, blends of Royal Jelly and honey were developed. In these products the Royal Jelly is combined with the honey to make it pleasant to take, and with other ingredients, such as bee pollen and extra vitamin C, to enhance its composition. It can be taken by the spoonful.

I remember that when I was a child I used to steal spoonfuls

of sugar or jam, and I would guess that few of you could put your hand on your heart and deny that you had a craving for sweet things when you were tiny or say truthfully that you never transgressed, as I did. Perhaps if Royal Jelly and honey had been available then and if my parents' generation had known as much about nutrition as we do today, I might have been treated to a spoonful of Royal Jelly each day instead of waiting till my mother was out of the way and making for the cupboard.

There is a variety of Royal Jelly and honey products on the market and, since this is the easiest medium in which to preserve fresh Royal Jelly, most of them contain the pure substance. There is also a tremendous variation in price from brand to brand, and so the choice can be bewildering when you first look at the range on the shelves of your health food store.

The price is usually related to the amount of Royal Jelly contained in the product. This is always stated on the jar and can range from 3.5 to 20g. The total contents of the jar will also appear. If this is, for example, 290g and the product is intended to last thirty days at one spoonful per day, then you will be taking about 10g of tonic per day. If the Royal Jelly content of the jar is 3.5g, then your daily dose of Royal Jelly will be about 120mg. Similarly, if the jar has 10g of Royal Jelly in it, then you will be getting roughly 330mg per spoonful. Compared with the capsules, that is quite a big dose of this protein, mineral and vitamin-rich substance. The beauty of Royal Jelly is that high doses can be taken safely, since it contains no drugs or toxic substances.

It is always wise to do exactly what you probably already do with your grocery purchases, and that is to check the quantity of product plus the quality of its content, against the price, to make sure you are selecting value for money.

It is true, of course, that today, children tend not to have quite such a sweet tooth as I may have had when I was young. These days, at a children's party, all the crisps, nuts and sausages-on-sticks seem to disappear and the sweet stuff is often left. This is, I believe, due partly to the gradual dissemination and acceptance of new nutritional values.

When my daughter was a baby, I recall chatting with an old lady in the doctor's surgery. A little ashamed that my offspring was rather too rotund, I was explaining that I had recently put her on a sugar-free diet. 'But where will she get her energy from?' asked the old lady, most concerned for her welfare. There was nothing I could say to persuade her that I was not depriving my daughter of essential nutrients. Thankfully, most young mothers and many of *their* mothers are better educated now, and are feeding their babies less refined foods. Hence, perhaps, the new 'savoury-toothed' youngsters of today.

Royal Jelly with honey is, however, versatile. If an unadulterated spoonful proves too sickly, then you can spread it on your toast or use it as a sweetener. In fact, you can, within reason, do what you like with it. The only thing to avoid is heating it, because that can destroy most of its nutritional value.

A world-class sportswoman, herself a dedicated Royal Jelly capsule fan, decided to let her family in on the act, and she writes,

> My eight and a half-year-old son . . . has also become a . . . Royal Jelly-boy — and within three weeks his appetite improved and he avoided the . . . succession of winter colds which in past winters endlessly interrupted his schooling.

Royal Jelly in capsule form or blended with honey, then, is designed to be taken on a daily basis, and really should be tried for at least three months before a decision can be taken whether to make a continuous Royal Jelly regime part of one's life.

Liquid Royal Jelly Pick-Me-Up
Fresh Royal Jelly is also available in high doses, in liquid form, as an instant pick-me-up. If you ever travel to the Far East, you will find such preparations on sale in a glass phial or

ampoule. What you're supposed to do is to break the end off and quaff the contents. I have never been able to bring myself to try this for fear that the elixir might literally be spiked with powdered glass! Another drawback of the Chinese products is that they contain alcohol as a preservative.

Fortunately in this country, and in many others, an instant liquid Royal Jelly energy booster, without alcohol, is now available in a neat phial with a screw cap, and it is drunk through a tiny straw — much more convenient, more natural, and, thank goodness, less potentially dangerous! The fresh liquid Royal Jelly is blended with herbs and is suspended in a honey solution, to make it palatable, and to ensure that taking it is a pleasant experience.

Besides the Royal Jelly, the other main ingredient is Ginseng. Most people have heard of this substance and are aware that it has been prized for centuries, yet few know precisely what it is or exactly what it is supposed to do. Perhaps this lack of knowledge is partly due to the advertising laws in this country and overseas; since Ginseng products are sold as foods and not registered as medicines, the manufacturers are not allowed to state or imply that they are of any medical benefit. Descriptions of Ginseng products therefore tend to be rather vague. I shall, however, try to put the record straight, whilst endeavouring to be as objective as possible.

Ginseng is also known as *Panax* because it consists of the roots of *Panax schinseng Nees*, a plant which comes from Eastern Asia and which is cultivated in China, Korea and Japan. It has an aromatic odour, tastes sweet initially and has a slightly bitter after-taste. It is an antiseptic and a sedative. It soothes and allays inflammation of delicate tissues, stimulates and improves gastric function and excites sexual desire. It counteracts mental and physical weakness, is useful in the treatment of neuralgia and improves muscle tone. Perhaps Ginseng is most famed for its reported ability to lift people out of depressive states associated with sexual inadequacy.

The other components of the liquid Royal Jelly preparation are: *Capsicum*, of a type which is cultivated in South America and Africa; *Serenoa*, made from the dried fruits of a plant grown in the southern United States; and *Damiana aphrodisiaca*, which consists of the dried leaves and stem of a Mexican plant.

Among them, these three ingredients boast an impressive list of therapeutic capabilities: reduction of flatulence; improvement of the peripheral circulation; treatment of neuralgia and rheumatism; toning up the digestive organs which have become weak through old age; increased ability of the body to get rid of excess fluids; treatment of cystitis; repair of body tissue; balancing of hormones; alleviation of depression, anxiety neurosis, dyspepsia and constipation; and improvement of sexual performance. To these must, of course, be added the beneficial properties of the elements of the Royal Jelly itself, which I have described in a previous chapter.

Unlike the capsules and the Royal Jelly and honey preparations, which are designed as part of a continuous health and fitness programme, a phial of high-dose liquid Royal Jelly is to be taken when required. It is, of course, safe to take it as well as a daily dose already taken in a different form. Like any other liquid preparation, as opposed to tablets or capsules, liquid Royal Jelly is absorbed relatively quickly by the body. Its effects are therefore felt quite soon after taking it — typically between thirty minutes and one hour.

What are these effects? Well, the product is intended to provide extra reserves of energy, stamina and concentration. People who take it and claim they derive benefit from it fall into two broad categories. The first consists of those whose levels of energy, staying power and mental alertness have been impaired through ageing or illness, and the second group are those who are healthy and young, but who need to call upon supplementary resources to cope with periodic activities which are extra to the normal daily routine and which are unusually taxing either mentally, physically, or both.

The Royal Jelly content of the product is 500mg per phial. As far as the elderly or ill are concerned, I have already mentioned the experiments with geriatric patients which have been carried out in Europe by the medical profession. Quite phenomenal recoveries from what had seemed to be hopeless senility have been effected with injected Royal Jelly. Appetites, the ability to think and express thoughts rationally and logically, and even the will to live itself, have all been restored in these patients.

Obviously, injecting a substance is the quickest way of getting it into the system. As far as commercially available Royal Jelly is concerned, however, oral intake of a liquid is the next best thing, for fast absorption into the body.

Many people who begin to feel that they are 'not as young as they used to be', find that Royal Jelly capsules or tonic can gradually restore their physical strength and stamina as well as their youthful outlook on life. If, however, the mental or physical exhaustion or weakness is severe, a phial a day of liquid Royal Jelly for a week or a fortnight is often recommended as a preamble to the capsule or tonic regime. Because the dose is high and because the effects can be felt more or less immediately, the subject receives encouragement, on the basis that the better you feel, the better your potential for further improvement. Once the capsule or tonic regime is subsequently established, then the Liquid booster is reserved for days which are going to be more demanding than usual.

On now to the young and healthy. Liquid Royal Jelly finds favour with busy people for all sorts of reasons. Again, testimonies abound as to its perceived benefits — and these concern business, sporting and recreational as well as social activities.

High-flying business people and showbusiness personalities who rely on liquid Royal Jelly have found that it can eliminate the problems of jet-lag, compensate for lack of sleep, and enable them to work more effectively and for longer periods. Sports people, both amateurs and professionals, have found that with a little help from the bees, they can train longer, concentrate their minds better, improve their performances and recover more quickly from the after-effects of excessive physical strain and mental effort.

It is no wonder that many of us take several days at the beginning of the annual holiday in the sun to settle down and enjoy ourselves, when you think of the preparation, the anticipation and the expense involved. Liquid Royal Jelly helps me, and many of my friends and acquaintances to get off the plane and into the Med without a second thought. Once you are back at your desk, or back at the kitchen sink, it can also eliminate that awful lethargic feeling of disorientation and dissatisfaction with life which can set in after an enjoyable holiday.

Some lucky people can take the social round in their stride, however hectic, but if, like me, you appreciate a little support when preparing an important dinner party or when having

Off the plane and into the Med without a second thought.

to sparkle in front of a lot of people you hardly know, then
liquid Royal Jelly can be of tremendous help.

Royal Jelly Cream

The external application of Royal Jelly is a relatively recent idea
to be exploited. Royal Jelly cream was originally launched as
a day or night face cream. It is blended with several other
ingredients which are known to be beneficial to the skin.

Natural vitamin E, for example, helps to protect and conserve
many other nutrients, and since the vitamin E content of our
food can easily be destroyed by exposure to air and light, by

freezing and by frying, a supplement of this vitamin is a good safeguard. Royal Jelly cream also contains jojoba oil for protection of the skin, and beeswax.

Since it was launched, all sorts of new market sectors have opened up and new uses discovered. It is now generally used as a body as well as a face cream and people have found it helps with dry skin, greasy skin, acne and sunburn, as well as with the more serious problems of eczema, dermatitis and psoriasis.

There are, as you can see, many ways of taking Royal Jelly, and there is no reason why the same person should not take it in all its forms. For example, I have been taking Royal Jelly capsules now for twelve years, and I feel they have given me good health, vitality and an ability to take the routine of my business and personal life in my stride. Sometimes, I spread Royal Jelly tonic on my toast. If I have a busy day ahead of me, then I take a phial of liquid Royal Jelly in the morning. Finally, I always use Royal Jelly cream under my make-up and I also find it very quickly soothes away any dry patches or skin blemishes which may appear from time to time. I have also included family pets in my Royal Jelly regime. There is a special form of Royal Jelly capsule available for animals, and, as you will see from a later chapter, I am not alone in my belief that their metabolism also benefits greatly from these additional nutrients. A glossy coat, healthy appetite and speedy recovery from illness are among the results I have observed in my cats.

Because more and more people are looking to natural ways of boosting their health levels, manufacturers of health products are continually reviewing the potential of traditionally beneficial substances and new discoveries. This has led recently to trials of 'combination' capsules which contain Royal Jelly and other complementary products, notably Oil of Evening Primrose. Briefly, this is the only readily available source of significant quantities of GLA (Gamma Linolenic Acid). Normally, the body converts fatty acids into GLA for the production of prostaglandins, which regulate all the major bodily functions.

No reason why the same person should not take it in all its forms.

This process is easily blocked, for instance by the intake of refined fats or too much alcohol, and by various common disorders as well as by the ageing process itself. Amongst the benefits of a direct intake of GLA are the relief of arthritis, improvement of the skin, and the alleviation of premenstrual tension.

In the health food market, new developments are taking place all the time. It's worth keeping up to date with what's going on, by reading the magazines, or simply by taking a closer look at what's on the shelves in your health food store.

References
1. R. Ardry, 'Contribution a l'etude de la gelee royale' (I, II, III, *Ann. Pharmac. Fr.,* XIV), p 97.

4.
FOOD FOR THOUGHT

Producing enough Royal Jelly for commercial sale is a significant problem in itself. Getting it from the hive and on to the health food store shelves is a complex and painstaking process involving care, expertise and specialized techniques.

Most of it comes from purpose built apicultural centres in China, although honey farmers and apiarists in this country are beginning to branch out into this field, too, even if the Royal Jelly produced is only in sufficient quantities for personal and family use.

In order to understand the basic production method, it is necessary to know a little more about the life of the bee colony, and because the bee's life history is unique, it took mankind many centuries to unravel the true story.

At the time of Aristotle, the one large individual which appeared to rule the colony was known as the 'King Bee'. It wasn't until the seventeenth century that Charles Butler, an English beekeeper, declared that the 'King Bee' was in reality a 'Queene'. I can imagine that this concept must have been quite a shock to a male-dominated society!

It was a naturalist by the name of Swammerdam who, in the same century, through years of devoted observation, revealed the strange truth, and that is that the one large individual is, in fact, the mother bee, and that, far from ruling the other bees, she is a slave to the process of reproduction. She is no more than a super-efficient egg-laying machine, working in perfect harmony with the workers who continue the rearing process, providing the offspring with food, shelter and care.

A hive *must* have a queen, and *one* queen only, and the colony is organized to produce a replacement as soon as the old queen stops laying or has been removed from the hive. It is rare for two queens to emerge at the same time, for preparation of queen cells and their occupancy is usually staggered to avoid this very occurrence. If it does happen, the two virgin queens fight to the death. As soon as a new queen emerges, she bites holes in any other queen cells to stop their development, and, if any of them contain nymphs, she stings them, making sure that she has no potential rivals. The observations of Francis Huber in his *Nouvelles Observations* after studying the emergence of a queen are quite graphic.

> Hardly ten minutes had elapsed after the young queen emerged from her cell, when she began to look for sealed queen-cells. She rushed furiously upon the first she met, and by dint of hard work made a small opening in the end. We saw her drawing with her mandibles, the silk of the cocoon, which covered the inside. But probably she did not succeed according to her wishes, for she left the lower end of the cell and went to work on the upper end where she finally made a larger opening. As soon as this was sufficiently large, she turned about to push her abdomen into it. She made several motions in different directions till she succeeded in striking her rival with the deadly sting. Then she left the cell; and the bees which had remained so far perfectly passive began to enlarge the gap she made, and drew out the corpse of a queen just out of her nymphal shell. During this time the victorious queen rushed to another queen cell and again made a large opening, but she did not introduce her abdomen into it, this second cell containing only a royal pupa not yet formed.

Huber goes on to describe how the workers mercilessly finish off the deadly but necessary task begun by the queen.

In the first few days of her new life, the queen makes several flights, only venturing a short distance at first, in order to learn the geography of the area. For, if she were to return to the wrong hive and try to enter it, she would meet her death. Then comes her 'nuptial' flight, during which a drone will catch her and mate with her. She stores his sperms in her sperm sac, returns to the hive and begins to lay eggs, and the young workers, known as nurse bees, are stimulated to produce Royal Jelly and to deposit it in the cells of the comb for the larvae to feed on.

For large scale Royal Jelly production, the queen is confined to the lower part of the hive, in a brood chamber. It must also be ensured that the colony is strong enough for efficient cell building and contains a sufficient number of young worker bees capable of producing Royal Jelly. In the absence of a hive mother, these workers set about the business of replacement, and this involves a significant increase in their production of Royal Jelly, which they deposit in the freshly started queen cells.

The time for harvesting a portion of the Royal Jelly is critical. On the one hand, the longer you leave the cell, the greater the harvest; the average yield from a two-day-old cell is 125mg, and that from a three-day-old cell is 225mg — an increase of eighty per cent. On the other hand, after the third day, accumulation slows down, and the quality of the Royal Jelly starts to deteriorate, as far as optimum nutritional content for humans is concerned.

The Royal Jelly is syphoned from the cells by means of a specially arranged syringe, and then filtered through fine cloth to ensure cleanliness and uniformity. It is then immediately refrigerated and kept at 4°C, until it is consumed fresh, encapsulated, or processed in some other way to produce the final consumer product.

It is probably true that Royal Jelly in its pure state is the richest natural substance available to us, in terms of the variety of nutritional elements it contains. These vitamins, proteins and minerals are, however, delicate. So many of them can be diminished, degraded or even destroyed, not only by processing of various kinds, including cooking, but just by simple exposure to light or air.

Scientists constantly search for preservation processes which minimize damage to the quality of original foodstuffs or pharmaceutical materials. Lyophilization is one of the best methods they have found. When I say that among the people who should be grateful for the development of this process are haemophiliacs and coffee drinkers you begin to get an idea of how widely the technique is used.

Lyophilization is a process by which a substance is frozen, treated with solvents and dried. It is used extensively in the pharmaceutical industry. Perhaps the most well-known item produced by this method is in the field of 'fast moving consumer goods', as they are known in the language of

Fresh from the hive is best.

marketing. To many people, instant coffee powder is not an acceptable substitute for real coffee. Yet the freeze-dried granular type enjoys wide acceptance, even among the snobbiest of coffee snobs. Lyophilization is, as the product label claims, the best way we have for capturing the goodness, flavour and aroma of ground, roasted coffee and presenting it for reconstitution by adding water.

Just as this process makes life more convenient for drug companies, the medical profession and patients, as well as for food processors, retailers and consumers, it also makes the task of turning fresh Royal Jelly into capsules a lot easier. Thus, there are several brands of freeze-dried Royal Jelly capsules on the market. In fact, for many years it was thought impossible to get the Royal Jelly out of the hive and into the capsule without first processing it. After a lot of careful research and technological development, the technique for doing this has been perfected.

The question remains whether this expensive and time-consuming research and development was all worthwhile. Scientists at the Honey Institute in the Department of Agriculture at the University of Bologna decided to find the answer to this very question.

In theory, freeze-drying should not cause any alteration to the constituents of Royal Jelly. In practice, however, changes do take place. None of the elements are actually lost, but the molecules which make up each substance become rearranged to form new structures, many of which are difficult to analyse. To summarize the findings, we can say that the sugars contained in Royal Jelly are degraded by freeze-drying, but, from a nutritional point of view, this is not really significant. More important is the degradation of the amino acids. This change in the Royal Jelly can actually be detected by taste. It takes on a light 'toasted' or 'caramel' flavour. Perhaps coffee drinkers with really sensitive tastebuds would say this about freeze-dried coffee, too!

With freeze-dried beverages, the customer gets two advantages — the first is price, and the second is convenience. Obviously these often outweigh the slight loss in flavour. With freeze-dried Royal Jelly, however, the consumer only gets the price advantage. It is the manufacturer who gets the convenience benefit.

One Royal Jelly user writes about capsules containing the *fresh* product,

> It is certainly far more effective than any of the freeze-dried royal jellies I have used before.

Only each individual can decide whether the loss of potency which freeze-drying causes outweighs the potential to save money.

However you decide to take it, Royal Jelly can, at first sight, seem expensive compared with some other products alongside it on the health food store shelves. Perhaps my description of the variety and value of its contents in an earlier chapter, and this outline of the knowledge, time, expertise, care and precision which go into gathering such minute amounts of the substance and delivering them to the consumer, will help existing as well as potential users to decide whether the relatively high price of Royal Jelly products is justified. It might also help to put things in perspective if you work out how much you spend per month on, say, newspapers and periodicals, or on coffee and sweets. Perhaps you might decide to spend that money on feeding your mind and your body with Royal Jelly instead!

5.
PANACEA . . .

Many a committed user of Royal Jelly would regard the substance as a panacea for his or her particular group of problems and requirements. Indeed, if you were to see all the letters which people have written to me in gratitude for Royal Jelly, and then make a list of the disorders which they feel Royal Jelly has remedied or alleviated, 'panacea' is probably the first word which would come to mind.

There is a growing body of opinion and supporting research which places diet supplement, adjustment and balance at the forefront in preventative and remedial medicine. I would recommend, especially for serious conditions, an individual assessment of each person's unique nutritional needs by a doctor or a consultant. The spectrum of nutrients which Royal Jelly covers, is, however, so broad that (a) it is not surprising that it helps in so many different ways, and (b) it is a good and safe starting point for the 're-balancing' process for most people, especially if one's family doctor is unsympathetic, or cost makes private consultancy out of the question.

Acne
This is a problem which commonly affects teenagers. It is also interesting that the condition can appear, or worsen, during times of stress and worry. Many women, too, get spots at certain times of the month, which they can relate to their menstrual cycle. The factor that these occasions have in common is that they are times when the hormonal balance is most likely to be upset. The amino acids, B vitamins

and vitamin C in Royal Jelly can be of significant help in improving the complexion and thus alleviating the distress which acne can cause. A lack of vitamin E is also implicated in this condition, and so the external application of Royal Jelly cream with added natural vitamin E is also a treatment to be considered.

Allergies

Generally, either people are aware of what triggers their allergic reactions, or with professional help the culprit can be isolated, so that treatment can be devised or if possible, the substance avoided. Recently, however, more and more allergies seem to be cropping up, especially those which affect the skin, for which the allergen cannot be traced. There are so many additives and chemicals in the food we eat and in the domestic products we use — and these can vary considerably from brand to brand — that it would be impossible to test for everything. Many acquaintances of mine have undergone the standard tests which have been developed, without any helpful results.

Identifiable or not, allergies have been kept at bay with Royal Jelly treatment — vitamin B_6, vitamin C and manganese being three of the active ingredients in this area.

Anaemia

There are several different types of anaemia, but the symptoms are well known: weakness, tiredness and a pale complexion. Iron, vitamins B_6, B_9, B_{12}, and manganese, all of which are contained in Royal Jelly, are particularly beneficial in improving the condition of the blood and hence its efficiency in transporting oxygen and nutrients around the body.

Angina

Gripping pain in the chest of this type is usually due to an insufficient oxygen supply to the heart muscle. It can be the sign of serious disease, and most people seek medical help when this warning sign appears. Royal Jelly has provided valuable assistance in reducing the pain, by improving the efficiency of the circulation and hence the condition of the heart itself.

Anorexia

This condition is usually associated with psychological problems, and must be treated with sensitivity. Royal Jelly does have a role, however, in stimulating the appetite and inducing controlled weight-gain. When I heard in the news recently that a woman had given birth to sextuplets and that the multiple birth was probably due to a side-effect of a drug which she had been taking for anorexia nervosa, my convictions about trying nature's remedies first, and only using drugs as a last resort were greatly strengthened.

Anxiety

A phrase which crops up again and again in reports from Royal Jelly users is, 'I find I can cope better with life'. It is not just our physical health which is governed by the chemical balance, or imbalance, in our bodies, but also our state of mind, our ability to cope with emotion and the efficiency of our nervous system. As many researchers have concluded, Royal Jelly has a marked effect on the secretion of various chemical substances in the body, and it would seem that calmness and relief from anxiety are benefits which can result from this action.

Arthritis

In both osteoarthritis and rheumatoid arthritis, it is the cartilage in the joints which is impaired. Vitamin C is particularly necessary for the maintenance of cartilage. Also, pantothenic acid and pyridoxine are constituents of Royal Jelly which play a part in the prevention or repair of damage.

As early as the 1960s, Dr Barton-Wright, a consultant microbiologist at a London Hospital, claimed that arthritis is a metabolic defect. As he increased the pantothenic acid level in twenty rheumatoid patients, so, in fourteen of them (70 per cent), mobility of the affected joints also increased. With thirty osteoarthritic patients, it took between four and eight weeks for them all to show a 'sudden and dramatic improvement'.

Asthma

The causes of this condition, and the circumstances which bring on attacks, can include hormonal imbalance, allergic reaction, anxiety and infection, all of which are factors which the ingredients of Royal Jelly help to correct or prevent.

Baldness

A friend of mine who was balding at the tender age of twenty-six asked his doctor for help. 'The only guarantee against baldness', said the doctor, 'is a father, two grandfathers, four great grandfathers and eight great great grandfathers, with a full head of hair each!' Of course heredity plays the major part in this, but claims that hair has begun to grow on heads which have been naked for years, following a period of Royal Jelly treatment, are not as far-fetched as they sound. Riboflavin, pyridoxine, inositol and biotin are all involved in the process of maintaining healthy hair, and indeed, an improvement in its condition is usually the first thing people notice when someone starts their Royal Jelly regime. So, although I doubt Royal Jelly will literally give you a complete new head of hair, it is possible that it could slow down the process of balding, just as it appears to slow down the ageing process itself.

Breathlessness

This may occur in any condition where there is a deficiency of oxygen or an excess of waste products in the blood. Royal Jelly's ability to improve the quality of the blood and its circulation can only be helpful in these circumstances.

Bronchitis

Inflammation of the lungs can be avoided by strengthening the immune system. In several scientific studies, as well as

in a host of more subjective accounts, Royal Jelly has been reported to do just that. Vitamin B_6 and the complement of amino acids are among the elements in Royal Jelly which also help chronic sufferers with tissue repair.

Cancer
It would be foolish to propose Royal Jelly as a cure for cancer, but I have one touching story to relate. A young Spaniard told me that when his mother was seriously ill with a brain tumour, she was in considerable pain and the doctors gave her a few months at the most to live. She began taking Royal Jelly capsules and achieved a level of well-being which made life actually worth living, and my Spanish friend believes that she owes what turned out to be *three years* of enjoyable life to Royal Jelly.

Among scientific tests in this field, American studies of the effects of Royal Jelly on tumour cells in mice produced encouraging results.[1]

Colds
Although many people who report their experiences often major on more distressing problems from which they have found relief with Royal Jelly, most of them, when questioned specifically about colds, say that they have had fewer than they did before taking Royal Jelly, and that those they have had succumbed to have lasted for shorter periods of time, and have not caused any serious disruption to their working and social lives.

Constipation
Contrary to the old belief that we should 'go' once a day, it is generally recognized now that we should open our bowels probably several times a day. The main criterion for health in this area of our daily lives is that we should perform easily without any strain or discomfort. We have other societies, less sophisticated than our own, to thank for our discovery that unrefined foods are an aid to the efficient and rapid

metabolism which promotes good health. The star nutrient which is lacking in highly refined food, and which has now been restored to us since the value of fibre has been acknowledged, is vitamin B_1. Royal Jelly helps to supplement any deficiency of this vitamin, now universally accepted as essential for good health.

Coronary disease
Naturally the success of Royal Jelly in treating heart problems depends to a large extent on the severity of the disorder, but it has been shown to help. Many now believe that our state of health as years advance is a consequence of our diet from the day we are born. Royal Jelly can be helpful in keeping our blood, our circulation, the blood-vessels and the heart in good working order for longer, thus preventing, or certainly delaying the onset of coronary disease.

Cramp
Cramp is generally the result of a poor supply of blood to the muscles. This can be due to a variety of circumstances, including arterial disease, exhaustion, cold, injury, excessive sweating, and the repetitive movement of certain muscle groups. Royal Jelly's beneficial effect upon the quality of the blood and the efficiency of the circulation helps to prevent cramps. Many sportspeople have readily testified that since starting on Royal Jelly, they have had no further problems with cramps.

Cystitis
Many people suffer this painful disorder from time to time, and it is more common in women. The increased frequency of urination and the pain this causes are brought on by infection and inflammation of the bladder. It is a complaint which must not be taken lightly, because it can lead to, or be the effect of, more serious problems. Mostly, the people who are affected can't wait to get down to the doctor's surgery and to get started on the antibiotics which they know will

Most people can't wait to get down to the doctor's surgery and get started on the antibiotics. Perhaps there is an alternative!

quickly clear it up. Even the medical establishment are beginning to discourage the expectation of automatic prescription of antibiotics for every disorder under the sun. One of their effects is a reduction in the body's ability to absorb and use the B vitamins, which, in conjunction with vitamin C and minerals, can be helpful in getting rid of cystitis. The following letter from a South Croydon housewife may give some sufferers encouragement.

. . . after two months' supply of Royal Jelly I am *free of cystitis completely*. I have been plagued with this *for five years*, and when a bad attack occurs I have to resort to antibiotics to clear it up. The severe attacks are frequent, and just recently I had been getting them once a month. You can imagine how delighted I am to have found a substitute for antibiotics.

Debility

If you lack energy and stamina, then it is likely that your metabolism is not functioning as well as it could. Naturally, people's capacity for a healthy metabolism varies and can be restricted by disease or impaired by the ageing process, but it is also true that nobody can hope to achieve his or her maximum potential if the nutrients and metabolites needed for energy are missing from the diet. So, a 'broad spectrum' supplement such as Royal Jelly can help in restoring and maintaining energy and stamina levels.

Depression

You've probably noticed how much I use the phrase 'mind and body', and really I find it rather senseless to talk about one without including the other. The idea of the brain governing what we do with our bodies is one which most people would take for granted. But the brain is an organ of the body, requiring oxygen and nutrients just like any other. Thus, *what we do with our bodies governs the brain*. Not only that, the brain is more complex than other organs as well as more sensitive to chemical imbalances. It might take a little time for some readers to take in the notion that our thoughts, behaviour, emotions and general state of mind are just the result of so many chemicals rushing about our bodies and reacting with each other in various ways. In fact the concept may conflict with some peoples' philosophy of life. If you think about it objectively for a moment, however, I think you will see that there is some truth in it. A wide variety of essential vitamins, amino acids and minerals, leading to a balanced metabolism should, then, lead to a healthier brain and nervous system which, in turn, should lead to a more balanced outlook on life. In order to climb out of a depressed state, it is that balance, that objectivity, which needs to be restored.

Dermatitis

This is a term used for many disorders which result in inflammation of the skin and it often covers eczema and psoriasis too. It can be brought on by specific contact with a variety of agents including substances contained in household products, different metals and certain species of plants and flowers. The inflammation, scaliness and itching can also appear for no *apparent* reason, and sometimes the onset or worsening of the condition can be connected with psychological or emotional events.

Because corticosteroid creams will often get rid of unsightly and embarrassing lesions quickly, it is tempting to use them. Longterm regular application of these is, however, already frowned upon by most doctors, and, after all, they do not strike at the roots of the problem. Whatever those roots are, a varied nutritional intake is going to help, and the vitamins B_2 and C in Royal Jelly will play their part. Vitamin E aids healing, and so external treatment with Royal Jelly and vitamin E cream could be a valuable additional treatment.

Dysmenorrhoea

Many women have found relief from period pains by taking Royal Jelly. Some corroboration of this effect also comes from Eastern Europe, where a more formal trial has been carried out. Out of thirty girls, all of whom suffered severe pain, only two failed to show any improvement after two months of taking a preparation of pollen and Royal Jelly. That's more than a 93 per cent success rate.

Dyspepsia

Generally speaking, if indigestion occurs frequently, at regular times, and causes a pain which can be specifically described, then this could be an indication of a serious disorder. Unless the discomfort is attributable to some medical problem, most of us usually blame it on an excess of one sort or another, or on the intake of something which 'doesn't agree with us'. Contrary to popular belief, a diet with plenty of fruit and vegetables can help to reduce the acidity in the stomach. Since the nutrient quality of this produce can be severely lessened during storage, Royal Jelly's vitamin C and B and minerals can be a useful ally in preventing and in relieving problems of this kind.

Eczema

It is probably not common to think of the skin as an organ of the body. Yet it is the largest, and one of the most complex in its physiology. The condition of the skin is an area of health care in which the potential effects of diet have long been recognized. However, most of the advice which has emanated from this approach has been negative, and has recommended the elimination of certain types of food. Of course, eczema is also often associated with nervous, psychological and allergic reactions. Eczema is undoubtedly a complex and, for many, a distressing condition. Yet, the delighted reaction of one mother to Royal Jelly is a pleasure to read.

My six year old son has always been a hyperactive child — sleeping little and burning up a great deal of nervous energy. He has always reacted to stress of any sort with attacks of eczema which varied in severity with the extent of his anxiety.

It was suggested that Royal Jelly might be able to help him but I was sceptical. As Royal Jelly can do no harm, I agreed to give it a try. At first there was no change but *gradually after ten days, the eczema faded* and didn't reappear and he was going to sleep when he went to bed and waking up much later. His appetite improved and he seemed altogether calmer. Friends have remarked on his change. Over the months the improvement has been maintained and there have been no further eczema attacks. I shall of course continue with the treatment as it would be wonderful to have this lovely, happy, eczema-free child remain cured.

Can a child of six feign response to this extent? I doubt it. I agree that his mother's diagnosis does not constitute an objective medical appraisal of his demeanour and behaviour, but his behaviour was obviously causing his family serious problems and they must have abated for his mother to write in this way.

Fatigue
How many of us experience, and complain of, tiredness? The famous 'post-prandial dip' — that awful drowsiness that comes over some people after lunch and which precludes them from

proper concentration in a meeting, or persuades them that the spring-cleaning can wait, is so common.

How often have we heard our friends tell us how they fall asleep in front of the TV, even though they have been looking forward to the particular programme for weeks? Problems of this type usually begin or worsen as we get older. Vitamin B_5, which is a constituent of Royal Jelly, is associated with the prolongation of life, and in tests, the adminstration of Royal Jelly has reduced fatigue in the elderly.[2] Fatigue can also be a symptom of many conditions which have been ameliorated by Royal Jelly treatment. 'Vitality' is a word which occurs again and again in letters from people who have found a new joy in life after starting on Royal Jelly. An American lady reports that after taking Royal Jelly for a few weeks, 'My friends started to notice that I didn't fall asleep on them at night while visiting.'

Haemorrhoids

I've never quite managed to fathom out why the subject of piles always seems to raise a laugh. I do know, by painful experience, that giving birth to two children can be a contributory factor to such problems. Temporary though my problem may have been, I can sympathize with sufferers of this complaint. It doesn't really help to say that a haemorrhoid is just a vein which has become enlarged and swollen, or to say that a change of diet may not help an advanced case. However, boosted amounts of vitamin C and E can help with prevention of renewed problems, and there is also evidence that vitamin B_1 helps to reduce the risk of constipation which, as sufferers will readily acknowledge, can aggravate the situation. Vitamins B_1 and C are contained in Royal Jelly. Tonics often contain added vitamin C, and Royal Jelly Cream with vitamin E is a candidate for external application. So, Royal Jelly products present a variety of ways to attack this far from amusing complaint.

A dedicated Royal Jelly convert in New York lists 'No more haemorrhoid flare-ups' among the benefits which Royal Jelly has brought to her life.

Hay-fever

It may seem strange to prescribe Royal Jelly, a substance which has pollen among its raw materials as a potential remedy for hay-fever which, for many people is triggered by flower or tree pollen. Yet, there is nothing to show that pollen taken by mouth has the same effect as exposure to pollen in the air. In fact, preparations based on raw pollen have been acclaimed by some as helpful for this condition. With such a wide variety of circumstances which result in the onset of an attack, from pollen to paint, and from dust to anxiety, it would perhaps be foolish to suggest any blanket prescription, but generally vitamin B_6, vitamin C and manganese have been shown to help with allergies generally, and when you read the following account, you may feel that Royal Jelly is worth a try. A woman from Weybridge writes:

> The course of Royal Jelly was a great success, as I found it greatly helped my hay-fever, and I was able to cut out anti-histamine tablets, except on the occasional days when I needed one tablet. I feel I started the course a month too late as my hay-fever is worst in April-May (tree pollen).

Headaches

A pain in the finger or the foot, and even, what my daughter euphemistically calls 'a pain in the arm' can be readily tolerated as long as it is not too severe! Yet a pain in the head seems to pervade the very consciousness. If headaches are severe, persistent and/or frequent, they can be a symptom of something serious. Many headaches which send people rushing to the medicine cabinet for an analgesic, however, are the result of tension of one sort or another. Vitamins B_1 and B_3, both of which are contained in Royal Jelly, have a favourable influence, physiologically and neurologically, which can relieve headaches of many types.

Hernia

Here again is one word for a variety of conditions. The factor they have in common is that one organ of the body or another has burst through a weak part in the wall which is supposed to contain it, to cause discomfort and pain. In the long term, if some types of hernia remain untreated, they can prove lethal. Many people do, however, live with, and put up with them for years.

The original weakness in the wall can be one which is anatomically quite normal, or it can be a slight deformity with which one is born, or it can be the result of surgery, illness or old age. Often the hernia is actually caused by the increased pressure which can be occasioned by chronic coughing, straining to pass motions or lifting heavy weights.

In Royal Jelly there are ingredients which help to maintain and repair body tissue, those which help prevent infection, and those which help prevent constipation. Between them, it is feasible that they could play a preventative role. As far as treatment is concerned, there is a body of subjective evidence to suggest that Royal Jelly can bring relief, which includes the testimony of this man from London.

(My daughter) persuaded me to take a course of four weeks' supply of Royal Jelly Capsules, in view of the constant pain I suffer . . . from a *Hiatus Hernia*.

It is now *almost three weeks* since the pain has virtually gone and as a daily sufferer for many years past you can well imagine my feelings of suddenly realizing that this was no coincidence but *a most incredible discovery for me.*

The most important event each day, is my pre-breakfast swallow of two magic capsules. Long may it continue!

Herpes

Herpes simplex, better known to most of us as cold sores, and usually associated with a cold or other infection, can cause embarrassment. Sufferers will readily vouch for the fact that they always seem to appear just before a special occasion when one would like to look one's best! It is a virus which remains in the cells and becomes active from time to time. Again, there is subjective evidence that Royal Jelly can help. In her long list of benefits derived from Royal Jelly in its various forms, the lady from New York, whom I mentioned earlier, says that she applied some liquid Royal Jelly to a cold sore on her lip several times a day and that in four days it was gone. Apparently she previously had to put up with these unsightly blemishes for about two weeks. This is, by the way, just one example of how users of Royal Jelly are constantly finding new ways of employing Royal Jelly products. Here, one which was designed for drinking has been used externally. I wouldn't, however, recommend a switch of application the other way round!

Hyperactivity

This is a word which has been, perhaps, a little too freely used since it was coined. Often, parents with a boisterous and energetic child, who needs less sleep than is convenient for the family, find that putting the label of 'hyperactivity' on the child helps, in finding the patience to cope with the extra demands placed upon them, and in explaining the child's behaviour to others. At one end of the scale, there are children in this group who would respond to a framework of discipline; they can be taught to modify their behaviour and to find solitary but engaging pastimes to pursue when others in the household need a little peace and quiet. At the other end are cases of children who genuinely cannot be tamed and whose metabolism differs from that of children we choose to regard as 'normal'. Traditionally in the West, we tend to look at a disorder, or often just one symptom of it, and apply something which will suppress that symptom. In my view, this is no way to approach the hyperactive child, or, for that matter the distraught parent. Tranquillizers bring with them the risk of side-effects and, although they may calm a few troubled waters, there may still be turmoil beneath the surface.

Royal Jelly, because its action is to balance the metabolism, has been shown to increase the capacity for renewed physical and mental activity, especially in the elderly, *and* it is also acclaimed for its calming effect. There are many grateful parents who have found that Royal Jelly has brought their offspring's behaviour within acceptable bounds of normality, and this even applies to the newborn.

Hypertension/Hypotension
Whilst I'm on the subject of balance — because of our conditioned attitude to treatment and our long acceptance of reversing an unwanted trend in the body with a specific drug which will suppress it, someone with high blood-pressure, who hears that Royal Jelly has helped *increase* blood-pressure in another patient, could be forgiven for dismissing this treatment as potentially harmful in his own case.

However, Royal Jelly has been shown to have a normalizing action, regardless of the conditions and trends it meets when it enters each individual organism. Just as it can re-awaken latent energies and enthusiasm for life in the depressed or suicidal, whilst modifying unacceptable behaviour in the hyperactive, so too can Royal Jelly raise the blood-pressure in those suffering from *hypo*tension, whilst lowering blood-pressure in the *hyper*tensive.

Impotence

Although, strictly speaking, the definition of impotence is the inability of the *male* to perform sexually, I should like to include women in my discussion of this problem. Sexual desire and sexual satisfaction in women are subjects which have only recently been aired, but I believe it is safe to say that lack of these can be equally distressing for either sex.

Although 'impotence' can be the result of disease, and in these cases once the disease is successfully treated sexuality should return, the vast majority of cases are psychological in origin. They result from feelings of anxiety of one sort or another. 'Anxiety is,' as my medical encyclopedia puts it, 'the most potent *anaphrodisiac*'.

Royal Jelly's action is biological rather than chemical and I have already spoken of its demonstrable ability to stimulate glandular secretion and hormonal activity. According to the French Doctor of Science and Pharmacy, Dr Ardry, Royal Jelly acts on the *suprarenals*.[3] These are glands just above the kidneys which pour their secretions directly into the bloodstream. They secrete *cortin*, a hormone which is concerned with carbohydrate metabolism and sex functions. They also secrete adrenaline following emotional disturbances such as fear, anxiety and anger, causing many physiological changes to take place, such as accelerated heartbeat, increased blood-pressure and increased output of glucose by the liver. Since Royal Jelly activates these glands which are of such vital importance to the life processes, the implications for Royal Jelly as a healer are very far-reaching.

Although 'impotence' is essentially a temporary problem, the anxiety which leads to failure is compounded by that very failure and a cyclic pattern establishes itself — success becoming more and more elusive. It would seem that Royal Jelly can help in two ways — by reducing the original anxiety, *and* by improving performance through an increase in appropriate hormonal activity.

Naturally, not many people volunteer anecdotes about their sex lives, but there is a report in a scientific paper from France which underlines the connection of 'impotence' with the psychological state and lends weight to these theories.

> A woman fifty years old, whom menopause five years earlier had left unbalanced, was suffering from nervousness, continual headaches, spasms of the throat, insomnia, backaches, fainting spells and a desire to commit suicide. After only six injections (of Royal Jelly) she forgot her ideas of suicide, became interested in her daily work, had no more difficulty in sleeping, and led a normal sex life. Her nervous tension disappeared.[4]

Insomnia

There are many people who worry unnecessarily about sleeplessness; just because most people are happy with the usual arrangement of between six and eight hours sleep at night, if you need less sleep or prefer to sleep at unorthodox times of day or night, and if you feel well on your regime, then there is no cause for anxiety. The only significant side-effect might be inconvenience for yourself and others. Trying to bend your natural individual circadian rhythm to fit in with the accepted pattern could cause more problems than it may solve.

Insomnia may, of course, be the effect of other disorders. If you suffer physical pain in, say, arthritic joints every time you try to turn over in bed, then the chances of having a good night's sleep are minimal. There are many painful disorders in this list which Royal Jelly has alleviated. Therefore if it is pain which is preventing you from sleeping, Royal Jelly is a strong candidate for consideration in the range of treatments available.

A man in Northampton, who couldn't sleep right through the night because of arthritic pain, had only been taking a daily capsule containing fresh Royal Jelly and Oil of Evening Primrose for five weeks when he reported his first good night's sleep in years.

Anxiety is also a major cause of lying awake at night. For some people, worries are genuine and severe; for others, relatively minor problems assume inordinately large proportions in the 'small hours'. Both circumstances are powerful in preventing sleep. Lack of restful sleep then reduces our ability to work out effective solutions, and so a vicious circle is set up. Royal Jelly has helped. Manganese and vitamin B_6 are known to have a tranquillizing effect, and both are contained in Royal Jelly.

Another 45 year-old Northampton man, taking part in a trial of the Royal Jelly with Oil of Evening Primrose product, stated that whereas before treatment he had been waking up several times during the night and finding difficulty in getting off to sleep again, after only a few days on his new regime he was managing to sleep right through *and* get up early without feeling tired.

Malnutrition

This is not a problem which many of us face, but in third world terms Royal Jelly treatment could be of great importance in this field. The findings of several paediatricians in France and Italy have proved it to be of great benefit in treating malnourished infants.[5] Their favourable results with premature babies have more universal significance.[6] Royal Jelly treatment has also been shown to compensate for malnourishment caused by lack of appetite in the elderly and infirm.

It is perhaps hard to believe that there are cases of malnutrition in our own society. Through over-indulgence, children occasionally receive such a monotonous diet that their metabolism and general health suffer. An acquaintance of mine told me, about her four-year-old son, 'I can't get him to eat anything else but fish fingers.' With another friend's six-year-old, it was toast and marmalade. A Royal Jelly supplement might well appeal to children who plague their parents with such extreme likes and dislikes, and it would certainly augment the range of nutrients in a child's diet.

Muscular dystrophy

This is a genetic disorder, the severity of which only sufferers and their families can appreciate. It affects the motor centre of the brain and is characterized by progressive deterioration and wasting of the muscles, which at first affects the gait and subsequently makes walking difficult or even impossible. Again, there are many forms of the disorder, and the most common type affects about 30 people in 100,000. I make no claims for Royal Jelly in this context, yet I received this letter from a woman in Blackpool:

> My daughter and I have both used . . . Royal Jelly capsules for over a year now and find them extremely good. We are both sufferers from muscular dystrophy and thought we would try them to see if they would help our condition. We have both felt better, also we were free from colds last winter. We have to be careful of chest colds in this complaint. My daughter also finds they help her have easier periods . . . These capsules are an expense we think is well worth taking.

Nausea

Nausea, with or without actually vomiting, has many causes, both physical and psychological. Acute fevers often begin this way, various abdominal conditions can cause it, including pregnancy, and it can also be caused by irritants to the stomach, including many drugs.

Nausea is a side-effect of many established drugs, the commonest of these being Aspirin, especially if it is taken on an empty stomach. Perhaps many of the symptoms and conditions for which we take drugs would be avoided if more of us insisted on a balanced intake of essential nutrients.

As far as the notorious morning sickness during pregnancy is concerned, this is just part of the package which many women have come to accept as part of the deal. Yet this, along with all the other problems which can occur at this time, such as sleeplessness, fatigue, depression, debility, cramps, numbness and, perhaps worst of all, irrational behaviour, can be as distressing to the woman as to the rest of her family. Many mothers-to-be, who, sensibly, have rejected the possibility of taking drugs for fear they may harm the foetus, have found safe relief from this general malaise by taking a daily capsule of fresh Royal Jelly.

It was, for example, widely reported in the national and international press that the Princess of Wales, having suffered a fairly miserable pregnancy with her first-born, shone with radiance, happiness and health throughout her second pregnancy, during which she took fresh Royal Jelly each day. As all mothers and fathers will know, no two pregnancies are alike, and such reports may be put down to journalistic whimsy, but so many women are convinced of Royal Jelly's efficacy in this area, that it is unlikely to be just coincidence.

The danger of vomiting, if it is excessive, is that the consequent loss of water and minerals can result in dehydration. In pregnancy it is particularly important to take in and to retain a varied and balanced supply of nutrients, and so Royal Jelly can be doubly beneficial. It will supply nutrition for mother and baby which may be lacking in the diet or lost through vomiting. It may also, if the subjective evidence available is anything to go by, actually help to prevent nausea and sickness in the first place.

Neurosis

Most of us are neurotic to some extent. I doubt if many people could honestly say that they have not at one time or another said to themselves, 'If I do this, then . . .', or 'if I don't do this, then . . .', or (more fatalistically) 'if such-and-such happens, then everything will be alright', or alternatively 'if such-and-such happens, then the thing I am most dreading will actually take place.' This type of neurotic behaviour is, however, relatively harmless as long as it is not taken to excess.

There are other more serious examples of neurosis which we may actually fail to recognize. For example, we will say that someone is 'obsessed with cleaning the house' or is 'obsessed with their work'. As long as these 'obsessions' are just exaggerations of our preconceived ideas of 'normal' behaviour, they remain acceptable and often even attract praise.

Neurosis only receives attention and becomes acknowledged

as a disorder when it causes behaviour which affects either the person concerned or the people around him or her, in an adverse way.

The anxiety which gives rise to neurotic behaviour can be the result of a variety of feelings such as inadequacy, guilt, fear, regret and resentment. Traditionally, psychiatric treatment may be given, and tranquillizers may be prescribed to suppress the symptoms. My medical dictionary says, 'There is no such thing as a nerve tonic.' Dr Destrem, an honours graduate in Medicine of the University of Bordeaux has, however, according to a report by his colleague Dr Chauvin, achieved spectacular results with Royal Jelly in the treatment of neuro-psychosis. [4]

Some of the young people whom he treated had ideas of suicide, others had obsessions, melancholia and nervous tension. Many had previously been treated in more traditional ways. The results Dr Destrem obtained were described as 'immediate and quite spectacular'; the patients gained weight, began to sleep normally and regained their usual health. Many of the medical trials I have mentioned involve only injected Royal Jelly. In this case Dr Destrem tried administering it orally too and 'the results seemed almost as satisfactory as by injection.'

It is likely that Royal Jelly's action on the glands restores the biochemical balance of all the organs of the body, including the brain and the nervous system. Perhaps this helps in allowing the patient to take stock, to take an objective look at his or her life and relationships with others, thus taking the first step towards adjustment. This is what many psychotropic drugs do too, but unlike Royal Jelly, they often carry with them the risk of unwanted side-effects.

Pain

'I had no pain in my toes since last May'; 'since taking these capsules I have not suffered'; 'after the first ten days the pain had gotten better'; 'before, I always had tremendous backache'; 'it is now almost three weeks since the pain has virtually gone';

'all I had to look forward to was a great deal of pain and discomfort'.

All these are extracts from letters written to me by people who have tried many other methods of reducing pain and who have found their answer in Royal Jelly. The letters concern arthritis, headaches, a nervous disorder affecting the urogenital system, period pains, hiatus hernia, and what the writer describes as 'a rare incurable disease'. Whether the Royal Jelly is acting on the disorders themselves, whether it promotes secretions which actually suppress the pain, or whether there is a bit of both of these going on, is uncertain. The fact is that all these people were disillusioned and desperate after years of searching and now their quality of life has been restored.

Phlebitis
This term usually applies to a vein near the surface of the skin which becomes obstructed by a blood clot — a sort of mini-thrombosis. It may follow injury or infection. Among the nutrients which assist in keeping the blood and blood-vessels in a healthy condition are vitamins C and E. A regular intake of Royal Jelly can help to prevent conditions of this kind. If you already suffer bouts of phlebitis, Royal Jelly may also reduce the risk of further trouble and gentle massage with Royal Jelly cream with added natural vitamin E can soothe and alleviate discomfort. As for the swelling which usually accompanies this complaint, this may also be reduced by Royal Jelly's natural gentle diuretic effect.

Post-natal depression
Having a baby, especially one's first, is arguably the single most traumatic event which ever takes its toll upon the female system. After such a gigantic physical, mental, emotional, social and psychological upheaval, it is a wonder that the balance of any woman's mind and body remains intact. Throughout pregnancy and during the first few months of motherhood, the body seems to reorganize itself, directing most of its

energies to the welfare of the offspring, and neglecting that of the mother. Just when a woman has extra demands placed on her, both emotionally and physically, in trying to cope with a new role and a new way of life, the biochemical balance of body and brain is too upset to supply the necessary reserves. The B vitamins and other nutrients in Royal Jelly are helpful in restoring and maintaining optimum mental function.

I am not forgetting that a father can also suffer from depression after the arrival of his sons and daughters, for, apart from the physical experiences of the mother, he goes through everything which his lady goes through, especially with the first-born. In addition he may experience envy and jealousy which he may not identify, but which he may express in many ways. His problems may be aggravated if the baby cries a lot, disrupts the couple's sleep and is particularly demanding. Royal Jelly helps husbands regain their equilibrium too, and, at first via the mother and later in tonic form, it has been known to make babies much less fractious.

I have observed the most placid behaviour coupled with a bright-eyed alertness and awareness among breast-fed babies whose mothers have taken their daily dose of Royal Jelly throughout pregnancy, birth and motherhood.

Pre-menstrual tension
This is a disorder which has always been with us, but which has only recently been recognized as a genuine condition — a candidate for treatment. It is one of the few phenomena which physicians on the orthodox side of the medical fence have treated with dietary supplement. Among Royal Jelly's constituents, vitamin B_6 is a particularly important factor in menstrual regulation — not to be taken, as with a drug, *when* the problem occurs, but rather to be taken all the time, throughout the complete cycle. Gamma linolenic acid, of which Oil of Evening Primrose is the only practical readily available source, has also captured the serious attention of the medical profession in the treatment of PMT. In an informal trial of a Royal Jelly/Oil of Evening Primrose capsule — one a day for

three months — after twenty days, the reaction of the mother of one young girl of fourteen was unequivocal; 'For the first time in two years, my daughter has had her period without driving us all mad, and without missing several days of school.'

Psoriasis

'As an indication of how well my arms look, I went out the other day and bought a short sleeved dress.' To those who don't suffer from psoriasis, or have never heard of it, this statement may not seem world-shattering. To the woman who wrote it in a letter to me, this event was probably one she never thought she would be able to experience. This skin complaint is not dangerous, but it is unsightly and apparently itches like hell. The letter continues: 'no more hiding in corners hoping people won't see me having a quick scratch!'

No-one really knows the cause of psoriasis, but it tends to run in families and it usually worsens during adolescence and in times of mental stress. Cortico-steroid creams, tar ointments and fluoride-based preparations were once liberally prescribed, but at best the disappearance of the red scaly patches was temporary. Now regular use of these drugs is frowned upon by the medical profession, and at last skin specialists are approaching the problem through adjustment of the diet.

Vitamins B_1, B_2, B_6 and B_8 all play an important role in the maintenance of healthy skin. Another reason for Royal Jelly's success in treating psoriasis could be that it helps mind and body to cope with mental and emotional stress in better ways.

Respiratory disorders

Royal Jelly has been shown scientifically to improve the efficiency of the body's use of oxygen, and many people report that it has helped them with breathlessness.

Varicose veins

These are caused by the failure of valves in the veins to keep the blood flowing in the right direction back to the heart, and they can be very painful and unsightly. Relief from the condition is one of the most common which Royal Jelly users write to me about. I suppose that is not so surprising since about half the women and one in four men over forty suffer from varicose veins.

Is Royal Jelly a panacea or a placebo? Certainly I do not have the results of *double blind* clinical trials involving hundreds of people, which most doctors would demand before taking it seriously. What I do have is an overwhelming amount of subjective evidence to support my belief in its benefits. As you will see from my next chapter, it has also been shown to be beneficial to animals in a host of different ways, and that, to me, would seem to discount the placebo theory.

References
1. Gordon F. Townsend et al, *Antitumor Activity of 10-Hydroxy-2-decenoic Acid from Royal Jelly* (Presented at annual meeting of American Association for Cancer Research Atlantic City 1959).
2. H. Destrem, 'Experimentation de la gelee royale d'abeilles en pratique geriatrique' (*Rev. Pathol. Gener. Physiol. Clin.* 1956), p. 1641.
3. R. Ardry, 'Contribution a l'etude de la gelee royale' (I II III *Ann. Pharmac. Fr.*, XIV), p. 97.
4. R. Chauvin, 'Action sur les Mammifieres et sur l'Homme de la gelee royale' (*L'Apiculteur, Sect. Scientif.*, 101 Annee No. 4, 1957).
5. C. Sarrouy et al, 'Essai de traitement de huit cas d'hypertrophie grave du nourrisson par les extraits de gelee royale' (*Pediatrie* No. 1, 1956).
   P. Prosperi et al, *Sull'impiego terapeutico della pappa reale delle api negli stati di denutrizione della prima infanzia* (1° convegno nazionale per lo studio dell'applicazione dei prodotti delle api nel campo medico-biologico. Bologna 1956).
6. G. Malossi et al, *Osservazioni sulla gelatina reale nell'alimentazione degli immaturi* (ibid).

6.
. . . OR PLACEBO?

Again, I have no evidence which might be accepted as 'scientific', to *prove* that Royal Jelly *works* with animals, but I have tried to be methodical in my gathering of information from animal owners. I offer a collection of reports, many of them from breeders of show animals, who generally do not display the sentimentality to which some pet-owners may be prone, and whose observations are therefore probably as objective as you can get outside the medical or scientific environment.

Afghan. 20 months old. Nervous of people, ring shy, slight loss of coat.

2 capsules per day for 14 days.

Dog has shown improvement whilst in a crowd. Whereas he would cower behind me, he will lie quite contentedly amongst dogs and people.

Cocker Spaniel bitch. 8 months old. Very highly strung, fine coat which is not growing to full extent.

1 capsule per day for 28 days.

Day 7: Periods of calmness whilst indoors.
Day 14: Tends to sleep more during day.
Day 28: She is a different dog now. So very much calmer. Still slightly nervy but not anywhere near as bad as before treatment started. Training her for the show ring is now a pleasure and not a continual struggle. Coat has improved greatly. Ears are also dropping down.

Cocker Spaniel bitch. *2 years old. Will not calm down and rest for any length of time. Will not body up or grow sufficient coat.*

1 capsule per day for 28 days.

Although we see this dog daily, the improvement in her as regards a show dog is evident even to us. No longer are we sceptical as to the treatment's worth.

Old English Sheepdog. *6 months old. 'Leaked' when sleeping, very travel sick, poor coat, extremely nervous in traffic.*

2 capsules per day for 28 days.

Steady increase in weight. Does not 'leak' any more. Travel sickness disappeared completely. Coat much longer and thicker. Improving very much with noisy traffic — does not bolt any more when cars pass.

Borzoi. *4 years old. Sluggish.*

1 capsule daily for 28 days.

Activity rate good, general condition improving. Cardiff Championship show won his *first Challenge Certificate*. Eyes much brighter.

Borzoi. *13 months old. Nervousness.*

2 capsules a day for 28 days.

Day 7: Little improvement.
Day 14: Has tolerated ring craft slightly better. Showed a big improvement with female handlers.
Day 21: Improvement maintained. Stood very well at the Windsor Championship Show. Awarded Reserve C.C.
Day 28: Some improvement can be seen, is gaining more confidence at ring craft, but it's a slow process.

Poodle. *8 years old. Anorexia nervosa.*

1 capsule daily for 28 days.

Day 7: Eating well. 1 can of *Pedigree Chum*, 1 saucer of milk.
Day 28: Eating well — as much as I will give him. His nose has turned from dull grey to shiny black.

Borzoi. *3 years old. Overweight and lethargic.*

1 capsule per day for 28 days.

Day 14: No change.
Day 21: Far more energy when shown. Won B.I.S. Has lost weight.
Day 28: Really moving well and lost weight. Won yet another B.I.S. award. Once the treatment finished, reverted to old ways.

Borzoi. *5 years old. Lack of coat, moves badly in the ring when shown.*

1 capsule a day for 28 days.

No change in coat due to moulting. Moves better in ring. Tremendous energy. Won first prize when shown.

Italian Greyhound. *5 months old. Trouble with feeding — has not been able to adjust to food after weaning. Thin — lack of muscle. Very nervous of strangers. Given every kind of food known to man and beast — hand feeding — leaving 8 hour gaps between meals. NO SUCCESS.*

1 capsule every other day for 21 days.

Puppy's feeding improved. Shows interest in food. More muscle tone. More energy. Still nervous. Definite improvement since taking Royal Jelly.

Alsatian. *9 years old. Growing old, tired, arthritic and depressed.*

4 capsules a day for 6 months.

Good coat and muscle, very good appetite and better energy. (His owner adds 'It appears that Royal Jelly capsules are responsible for Kepler's improvement. I'm also giving them to a very young Alsatian (just over 1 year) to see if they will help him through the later years of his life by providing him now with an added dietary supplement to sustain his enormous energy'.)

English Mastiff. *2 years old. Nerves. This dog was winning well and at the age of 18 months went shy.*

6 capsules a day before food for 7 days.

There is a slight improvement in this dog's nerves. Regarding energy, we can hardly restrain him. And mating a bitch? He would mate 3 times a day, so it definitely works that way!

Scottish Terrier. *2 years old. Poor appetite which eventually led to poor condition throughout.* (I have tried cooked meat, tinned dog meat, all in one dog food. Nothing seemed to work. Never seemed to be hungry. Leads an active life. Very thin. Poor coat.)

1 capsule a day for 21 days.

He came back from his morning exercise on that day (21st day of treatment) and actually howled for his breakfast — something he has never done — I usually have to force him to eat. Gaining weight. Great temperament. Nerves good. Coat growing in abundance at last. Very hard muscle. Endless energy. Great appetite.

I am printing the final extract exactly as I first read it, because I admire, as I hope you will, the owner's sense of humour.

Breed of Dog: Dachshund
Name of Dog: Noodles
Age: 10 years
Specific Disorder(s): Weak bladder
Remedies Previously Attempted: Water-proof knickers.
Dosage: 2 a day
Time Administered: 10am and 6pm

Progress at Day 8
Height/Weight: No change
Fertility: Lacks material
Temperament/Nerves: Hard to say
Coat: Glossy
Muscle: Tail wags strongly
Energy: Boy oh boy
Movement/Work Rate: Sleeps like a log
Appetite: Eats anything
Bowel/Bladder Function: See our carpet
Incidental Reports: Material improvement in all departments apart from sex impulses

In addition to these cases, for which I requested a formal report in the form of a questionnaire, there have also been many spontaneous reactions. Here are some of them.

My dogs are exceptionally beautiful in appearance and superior to other German Shepherds I have seen. German Shepherds I have had in the past, *not on Royal Jelly* have been almost dangerous. I definitely attribute my dogs' excellent temperament to Royal Jelly.

My West Highland Terrier bitch called Tammy . . . is 8 years old and has always been a very nervous dog, suffering from nervous eczema, especially on her stomach and paws.

On taking the (Royal Jelly) capsules regularly she has made a dramatic improvement. Her skin and coat are now completely clear from any inflammation and her nervousness has disappeared. She welcomes everybody happily and is far more alert and brighter than she has ever been before.

We have a young Scottish Terrier bitch which has been winning reasonably well but she did not seem to have the verve and confidence to obtain the maximum results in the ring. After giving her the recommended dosage we noticed a different approach in the Show Ring and a general improvement. As all other conditions remained the same, diet, vitamins, training and grooming, we attributed the change to the Royal Jelly capsules. Therefore we decided to give a course to all the stock and the puppies.

The most noticeable improvement in Ula was her coat. It has thickened-up lovely and in an Old English a good coat is important. She now does *Dulux* promotions for ICI. We are very pleased with Royal Jelly.

Zebedee, our Irish Setter, was an 'old man'. He was grey round the muzzle, stiff in the legs, had a dull coat and definitely didn't want to go 'walkies'. Two Royal Jelly capsules in his *Chum* each evening for the last two years, and he's like a puppy — alert, bright-eyed, intelligent, glossy-coated, and, after two long walks a day, he still asks for more exercise. The rheumatism has totally disappeared, and everybody notices how marvellous he is at the ripe old age of ten.

It is quite obvious that there are recurring themes throughout these reports — the main one being that of nervousness, an inability to behave as the owner would wish. In all cases there has been an improvement, a calming effect and an ability to cope with events which the animals previously found threatening. Another frequently reported result of the Royal Jelly regime was an improvement in the animals' coats.

There is a striking example of the 'two-way normalizing effect' which has also been observed scientifically, as well as anecdotally, in humans. Several dogs found their appetites with the help of Royal Jelly and one managed to lose weight. The excessive energy of some dogs was curtailed, whilst another animal was roused from lethargy.

Other problems which were alleviated were incontinence, travel sickness, eczema, senile depression and sleeplessness. It is interesting to note that, apart from the incontinence, these are disorders and problems which we have already met, and which have received help from Royal Jelly, in humans.

It is true, and regrettable to many people, that the metabolism of dogs is similar to our own in many significant respects. This makes them perfect subjects for trials of many products. I can sympathize with those who decry experimentation using dogs for testing products which might be described as frivolous, but we owe an inestimable debt to the canine species, and also to rats and guinea pigs for that matter, as far as medical trials are concerned which have resulted in safe products which have genuinely helped the human condition.

Returning to our animal reports, there are two phrases which are of particular significance — 'It's a slow process', and 'Once the treatment finished, reverted to old ways'. Royal Jelly, or any other product which forms part of a serious attempt to improve general health levels by balancing the diet, is not a 'cure' to be taken from time to time when things seem to be getting on top of you. For two-legged creatures, as well as four-legged ones, health through nature must be regarded as a new regime for life.

You will notice that some of these dogs began to show signs of improvement quite quickly. Even if you make allowances for statements like 'slight improvement' after seven days of treatment (where I grant that the owners may be indulging in a little optimistic wishful thinking), the temperament and health of all twenty-one animals were better after a month. I have also heard many *people* say (about their own condition), 'I noticed the difference straight away'. Here again, it may be that the decision to start on Royal Jelly is actually just one element in a newly adopted more positive approach to life, and this perceived sense of well-being may have as much to do with the subject's effort to pull himself up by his own boot-straps as it has to do with Royal Jelly. The time it takes for each individual person, or dog, to re-balance the system depends to a large extent on how far that system is out of kilter in the first place. Generally it takes time.

We can also take a lesson from the owner of Kepler the Alsatian. Royal Jelly helps to repair damage and restore good health, but it also helps to *prevent* damage and *maintain* good health. Why wait till systems begin to break down to try it? Try it, and if, within a reasonable period of several months, it brings noticeable benefits, carry on. Gradually those beneficial effects will become permanent features of life and further improvements will begin to emerge. With diet supplement, there is no such thing as tolerance or diminishing effect, as with many 'conventional' medicines. You may well 'get used to' feeling better, or to your pet's good condition and behaviour, but there is no way that the metabolism will 'get used to' what you're giving it and cease to respond.

Another informal trial I have carried out has been with horses.

Pepper — this 23 year-old pony had a stick wedged across his back teeth. The throat became very swollen and his breathing became very difficult. He was unable to eat or drink.

After 9 days on 5 capsules a day, his appetite was improving and his breathing less laboured.

Lark — this 7 year-old mare had a poor appetite and was taking a day or two to settle after a day's hunting.

After three months on 10 capsules a day, her appetite was better, she was definitely calmer and she was hunting well and really fit.

I followed the progress of another horse, **Rainmaker**, quite closely over a six month period. When he began on 10 × 100mg Royal Jelly capsules a day, he was lame, highly strung, aggressive and impossible to handle. Here are some extracts from his owner's comments.

Day 14: Vast improvement. Still jumpy, but now puts his ears up when someone goes into the stable and allows them to catch him easily.

Day 24: He is generally much calmer and more friendly and is starting to trust people. He is rapidly becoming a completely different horse.

Day 28: Still improving. Managed to pull his mane quite easily (he's always had to be twitched before). Have been schooling on the road with excellent results, because he is not so jumpy.

Day 49: He got tied up in wire yesterday but instead of panicking he allowed me to cut it off. Coat is looking super now.

Day 55: Yesterday I took him to an indoor school. He kept calm and was easy to hold. He was popping over 3' 6" without any fuss. Normally he gets very excited.

Day 69: Going very quietly and calmly. Was third in the Open Topscore. Coat looking really good. Very calm in the stables and also to school.

Day 71: He's really improved in his temperament.

Day 91: He did not have any Royal Jelly for two weeks and during this time he started becoming very aggressive again. I got the new supply last weekend and started feeding them immediately but he is still quite bad in the stable and attacked me a couple of times on Wednesday. His coat is still lovely and very shiny.

Day 98: He has improved a lot since last week and is now much quieter in the stable. His coat is still very shiny and sleek.

Day 105: He is looking so well now and is really keeping to the weight at which he is really marvellous. I was away and he behaved himself really well with the girl who looked after him and rode out really quietly.

Temperament and appetite, as well as recovery from injury are the themes which emerge. The fact that Rainmaker began to revert to his 'old ways' when the treatment was left off for a while underlines the necessity to regard Royal Jelly as a continuous regime.

These reported results with animals point to the fact, in my opinion, that Royal Jelly does genuinely improve the condition of mind and body. 'Auto-suggestion' and the 'placebo effect' are phrases I often encounter, when I enthuse about Royal Jelly. This cannot apply to our dumb friends. Without exception, these animals were unaware of any change in their diet. Yet, the evidence that Royal Jelly effected significant improvements is overwhelming.

7.

THE GREAT BALANCING ACT

Roughly three-quarters of a century since the purpose of Royal Jelly and its means of production in the hive were discovered, researchers are still grappling with the question of its precise composition, and the minute detail of its method of action on the metabolism. Whilst they pause over such problems as just what that unidentified four per cent of its composition is, or the analysis of *'the lipid fraction, hydrocarbons and sterols'*[1] or *'the effect of Royal Jelly on the oxygen consumption and on the activity of adenosine-triphosphatase in guinea pig tissues'*[2], doctors and practitioners in the front-line are getting on with the job; hospitals and clinics in some countries already use Royal Jelly as the preliminary treatment for all patients, regardless of the specific nature of their condition or disorder.

I am by no means denigrating the academic approach. If apiologists had not been curious about the phenomenal growth, reproductive capabilities and longevity of the queen bee in the first place, then Royal Jelly would not be available to us today, and the world would have been a poorer place for that. No, the research must go on; with each scientific paper which is written, a little more is added to the body of knowledge about the substance. As a result, medical practitioners and practitioners of alternative (or, as I prefer to call it — 'complementary') medicine are encouraged to try it in new areas of therapy.

Although a definitive explanation of how and why Royal Jelly works is probably still a long way off, extensive and prolonged observations leave no room for doubt that it is of benefit to

mankind and, unlike many drug-based therapeutic programmes, the Royal Jelly regimen is completely without unwanted side-effects.

I have spent a whole chapter describing the nutritional content of Royal Jelly, to demonstrate the wealth and variety of elements in this natural 'cocktail'. The fact that it has been successfully prescribed as a remedy for disorders as diverse as depression, psoriasis, arthritic pain and anorexia seems to justify the belief that nutritional deficiency in our diets is a major contributor to ill-health.

One of the remarkable aspects of the effects of Royal Jelly is what I call, rather unscientifically, its 'two-way normalizing action'. For example, for some it helps with insomnia, enabling them to get a good night's sleep, whilst for others, it helps with fatigue and drowsiness, preventing them from dropping off all the time! For some, Royal Jelly helps to calm overactivity of mind and body, allowing them to put things into perspective, whilst for others it provides the helping hand which lifts them out of lethargy and inactivity, putting the vitality and energy back into their lives.

This is the point at which I expect the sceptics to leap in and compare Royal Jelly with those bottles of foul-looking and worse-tasting liquid which were at one time sold by pedlars as concoctions which would cure everything from cardiac arrest to corns, from haemorrhoids to house-maid's knee.

No, Royal Jelly is not a cure-all, not a miracle-worker, and certainly not a concoction of doubtful origin! The key to understanding how it can act on the body in *seemingly* opposite ways is to regard it as a catalyst which, by restoring and maintaining the levels of essential nutrients, balances the system and improves the metabolism.

The important thing to remember is that the healthy, in-balance human body is a highly efficient self-healing unit. It has the capability to fight diseases, repair wounds and generate the energy and vitality essential for a meaningful and enjoyable life. The problems begin to occur when the chemical balance is lost. The *symptoms* of ill health which result can often be treated by drugs, but this will not remove the *cause*. One natural remedy is to bring the body back into balance with the use of a diet supplement such as Royal Jelly. To reduce Royal Jelly's effects to a list is probably to do it an injustice. Any such categorization is bound to be incomplete, but here goes! Here are just some of the ways in which people who prescribe it regard Royal Jelly.

A stimulant of appetite.

A weight regulator.

An aid to efficient digestion.

An anti-depressant.

A stimulant to glandular secretion.

An accelerator of the metabolism.

An antibiotic.

An immunizer against disease and infection.

A normalizer of sexual functions.

A promoter of healthy skin and tissues.

A natural, potent source of nutrition, supplementing the diet with important vitamins, amino acids and minerals.

If we look at Royal Jelly in terms of its ability to stimulate proper growth, replacement and repair, it has been used in all age-groups with success.

In the field of paediatrics, Royal Jelly has promoted weight gain in malnourished and underweight babies, bringing them up to levels which are regarded as normal and giving them a better expectation of long and healthy lives. For example, in the Department of Clinical Paediatrics at the University of Florence, forty-two children, including premature babies, undernourished children and those suffering from spasms were treated with Royal Jelly. The reports included the following results:

Appetite stimulated in almost all cases.

General visible results became apparent after twenty days' treatment.

Red corpuscles were increased and, in cases of hyperchronic anaemia, the different kinds of white corpuscles were normalized.

Assimilation of protein into the bloodstream after treatment was greater than that induced by any other known product tried in malnutrition cases. [3]

Increase in appetite, weight-gain, improved blood count and better defence against infection were also reported in another test, involving eight cases of extremely undernourished children. One of the doctors involved, Dr Quadri, described the results as 'brilliant' with four of them, and 'good' with three, after only two weeks of therapy. The seven children who did respond had, with the help of Royal Jelly, overcome an inability to metabolize fats.

A third study involving serious malnutrition in infants resulted in significant weight-gain, the disappearance of a 'drawn' look in the patients' faces, and the restoration of colour to their cheeks as well as brightness to their eyes. Although no controlled clinical trials have been conducted with people undergoing the often painful stage of adolescence, a mass of anecdotal evidence points to Royal Jelly's stabilizing effects during this period of life.

At the other end of the spectrum, geriatric patients with severe debility, lack of appetite, and disorientation due to senile dementia have Royal Jelly to thank for a new lease of meaningful life. In France, Dr Destrem treated a group of patients between the ages of seventy and seventy-nine with Royal Jelly. All of them were emaciated, senile, and deprived of physical strength. He recorded improvement of appetite and sensations of well-being in all of them within twelve days. He also stressed that in those patients whose blood-pressure was below normal, a significant improvement occurred. In normal and hypertensive patients, however, there was no increase.

In Russia, a country where a great deal of interest has been shown in Royal Jelly, Dr Kadyseva also reported the normalizing of blood-pressure — that is, an increase of blood-pressure in hypotensive patients and a lowering of blood-pressure in the hypertensive. He added to this observation that pain due to severe arteriosclerosis disappeared. Another Russian physician, Dr Mishchenko, confirmed these results in his tests with elderly patients. He also found that diabetics showed lower blood-sugar levels.

Greater mental and physical stamina, improvement in neurological function, and alleviation of debility and depression are common results of clinical studies with Royal Jelly in the field of geriatric medicine. Since all these symptoms point to a severe breakdown of whole bodily systems, these results are an indication of the far-reaching power of Royal Jelly.

In younger adults, most ailments proclaim partial breakdowns of these systems, and so Royal Jelly therapy often brings not just an improvement, but complete repair and recovery. In his review of recent European research, R. B. Willson, Director of the American Honey Institute, concludes that:

> Royal Jelly has been demonstrated to be of great aid in the field of gerontology, a therapeutic agent in cases of neuropsychosis and a strongly positive aid in the treatment of serious cases of malnutrition in infants. Royal Jelly has a tendency to raise low

blood-pressure but not to increase high blood-pressure. It brings the feeling of euphoria. Its active ingredient is hormonal in nature, having a biological action on the glandular tissue, notably on the suprarenals.

Not only has Royal Jelly been demonstrated to increase the appetite, but it also helps the body to use this enhanced intake more effectively. Clinical studies have shown that it corrects digestive malfunctions and that it helps — to a greater extent than any other agent which has been tried, to promote the assimilation of proteins into the bloodstream for transport to where they are needed for growth, replacement and repair.

By talking of increasing appetites, I have probably set alarm bells ringing in the heads of those who want to lose weight or at least avoid the 'middle-age spread' which we are told can be so detrimental to our health. There is no need to worry. This is another example of my 'two-way normalizing' theory. At first it may seem paradoxical that, in adults, Royal Jelly can increase the appetite, yet help to keep you in trim. But actually its quite logical. If the metabolism is speeded up and made more efficient, this not only accounts for the incentive to eat more, it also means that the body is using up the nutrients it needs and expelling those it does not require as it should. In fact, young adults who take Royal Jelly often lose unwanted inches.

One of the elements in my list, and an aspect confirmed by Dr Ardry, a French military physician, is increased glandular secretion. This is, of course, a very complex area of physiology and involves practically every bodily function. Among the effects of this property of Royal Jelly are: improved muscle and neuro-muscular function; the balancing of blood-sugar levels; and improved tolerance of stress, especially during adolescence and the menopause.

Also related to its ability to stimulate increased glandular secretion is Royal Jelly's role in restoring or enhancing our sexual desires and performance, and in regulating our reproductive functions and capabilities.

Many women have found that a regular intake of Royal Jelly brings relief from menstrual discomfort and disorder, alleviation of nausea, cramps, tiredness and depression during pregnancy, and avoidance of the post-natal and early motherhood blues. In combination, the augmented amounts of various hormones which Royal Jelly promotes do accentuate our secondary sex characteristics. It is to this action that these beneficial effects on the menstrual and reproductive cycles are probably attributable.

Because of this apparent 're-balancing act' in this particular area of our physiological activity, there is considerable interest among therapists and practitioners in Royal Jelly as a fertility aid. It is, I suppose a logical course to follow, when you recall that in the hive, the worker bee's sexual development is arrested once she is taken off Royal Jelly, whereas the queen, whose 'royal' diet is maintained throughout her life, develops complex and super-efficient reproductive mechanisms, as well as the almost unbelievable fertility and stamina to lay twice her own weight in eggs each day!

There are in fact reports, again from France, of cases of women who had stopped menstruating and were deemed menopausal and who, after treatment with Royal Jelly, went on to bear more children. The uprated secretion of sex hormones by the adrenal cortex also explains the increased sexual appetite and improved sexual function which many Royal Jelly users report.

Finally, with regard to Royal Jelly's ability to help us live longer and more healthy lives, its antibiotic and bacteriostatic properties are important. When you think of the variety and number of diseases and infections to which the bee colony must be prone, it is quite amazing that the hive remains disease-free. It is no wonder, therefore, that people who take Royal Jelly also display increased immunity and defence against disease and infection. The tests which were carried out in this field of Royal Jelly research resulted in some quite astonishing findings. Cultures of four common bacteria were neutralized by Royal Jelly in one minute. In tests which were developed by the US Food and Drug Administration for verifying the potency of antiseptics and disinfectants, Royal Jelly performed better than some common carbolic acid compounds used for antiseptic purposes. This research, which was also scrutinized by the FDA would seem to corroborate reports that Royal Jelly reduces the incidence of disease and infection.

The potential of Royal Jelly as a general preliminary treatment when patients ask for help with physical and mental disorders of almost every kind would seem to be, because of its rich content, logical. At worst, medical practitioners will regard it as harmless, and, indeed even if they are not convinced of its potential benefit, at least they can rest assured that it will, unlike many first line drugs, do no harm. I suppose a word of caution is necessary here; I deliberately say 'of *almost* every kind', because there are rare allergies which may be triggered, if not by the Royal Jelly itself, then by some of the accompanying ingredients of the commercial products. Let me take an example. Coeliacs disease is a condition which affects about 0.01 per cent of the population of this country. They are allergic to the gluten in wheat. Some Royal Jelly capsules contain wheatgerm oil, which for most of us presents no health threat whatsoever, yet in a coeliac it *may* produce an adverse reaction. Generally, however, people are aware of their allergies, and so a quick look at the ingredients of any product will enable them to judge whether it is of any danger to them.

So, as I say, at worst, Royal Jelly products will be regarded as harmless to *most* of the population. At best, those practitioners who are convinced that our nutritional intake makes a major contribution to the state of our health will regard it as: a good start in getting the metabolism into balance; a powerful therapeutic ally in the battle to maintain a general health level which represents the maximum potential for each individual; a positive aid to the alleviation of many troublesome symptoms which affect mind and body; and in some cases, the key to a lasting cure.

Because Royal Jelly is composed of such a long list of diverse vitamins, amino acids, minerals and other metabolites, it is impossible to pinpoint a particular ingredient as the one element which brings a particular benefit to a single individual. As a complex substance acting on an almost unfathomably complex system Royal Jelly will, I hope, be the subject of continuing research and trial. In this way we will gradually be able to piece together the whole story, not only of Royal Jelly, but also of diet supplement in general as a serious approach to the restoration and maintenance of good health.

What we can already be sure of is that the unique Royal Jelly mix acts on the blood, the digestion, the muscles, respiration, the nervous system, the psyche and the whole metabolic process. Its harmonious composition appears to get all intellectual, emotional, mental and physical functions working together in harmony.

Most recently, Royal Jelly has been recognized as an aid to healing, recovery and recuperation. Whether debility or pain are brought on by deliberate or inadvertent over-exertion, by essential or elective surgery, or by injury, Royal Jelly has been demonstrated to speed up the progress of many subjects on their road back to normality. It has also relieved suffering to an extent that the taking of drugs, some of which undoubtedly help but which can also produce other unwanted effects, has been avoided.

It is the unanimous opinion of sympathetic yet serious researchers and observers that Royal Jelly is a valuable addition to the diet for practically everyone, from the frailest to the fittest. From premature babies to pregnant mothers, from the world-weary octagenarian to the world-class athlete, and from the lonely depressive to the gregarious workaholic. Almost everyone is concerned about his or her health. Some of us are desperately searching for relief from crippling disorders. Others are no less obsessed by discomfort of various kinds which, although, to the observer, may seem of a minor nature, can so easily and insidiously ruin any quality of life to which most of us aspire. As I have said, I should like to see the prescription of Royal Jelly more widespread as a reasonable blanket initial treatment. I must, however, be grateful that, even though it is often tried as a last resort, it is frequently then acclaimed as the sole agent which has produced the long hoped-for results after years of frustrating, and often painful, searching.

The prescription of adjustment to the diet in general, and of Royal Jelly in particular, is already widespread among so-called alternative practitioners. I find it encouraging that the medical establishment is also beginning to recognize this approach to preventative as well as corrective therapy. It is irrefutable evidence from research, by eminent people in their own field, which is helping to change doctors' attitudes. Take the following quote from Dr Ardry of the Establissement Central de Transfusion de l'Armee Francaise, who said,

> It has never been possible to duplicate the dynamic reaction of Royal Jelly . . . in human beings with injections of the same vitamins as are contained in Royal Jelly at doses sometimes 1000 times as concentrated.

As I stated in my introduction, the purpose of putting before you this compilation of information, testimonials and personal thoughts is to encourage you to try the benefits of Royal Jelly yourself. Remember, in its fresh state it is the most natural and effective diet supplement known to man, and nearly all who use it find a real improvement in the quality of their lives. So try it!

References
1. Research carried out in Italy by Giovanni Lerker et al.
2. This is just one of the many papers published by P. Peichev et al in Bulgaria. At the start of his report, Peichev summarizes the results of previous research into Royal Jelly thus:

> Royal Jelly is a complex biological product and a combination of active biological substances such as the vitamins of the complex B, amino acids, ferments, micro-elements, hormones. For the bee it is a stimulant of the anabolic process and of productivity. Used in tiny doses for animals and human beings, it acts as a reducing and trophic substance, it changes the reaction of the organism to allergic rhinitis and asthma, has a favourable action on inflammatory processes and wounds in people suffering from diseases of the urinary passages or of surgical diseases.
>
> By pharmacological researches royal jelly was found

to act on certain parts of the vegetative and central nervous system. It also has a non-specific and anabolic action.

3. P. Prosperi et al, *Sull'impiego terapeutico della pappa reale delle api negli stati di denutritione della prima infanzia* (1° convegno nazionale per lo studio dell'applicazione dei prodotti delle api nel campo medico-biologico. Bologna, 1956).

INDEX